Caught in the Web of Deception

Caught in the Web of Deception

DR. CHARLES FRALEY, M.D.
WITH BOB FRALEY

Copyright © 2000
Christian Life Outreach, Inc.
All rights reserved
ISBN - 0-9612999-4-0

Published by
Christian Life Services, Inc.
6438 E. Jenan Drive
Scottsdale, Arizona 85254

Printed in the United States of America

I acknowledge and am thankful for the many hours of scriptural and historical research completed the past 30 years that I can share in this book.

Contents

Introduction

Dr. Charles Fraley, M.D., and his wife, Marlene, R.N., have served the Lord on the mission field in Africa since 1974. First in Tanzania, and then in Kenya, East Africa. Dr. Fraley is the Medical Coordinator & Executive Director of a large health ministry in Kenya with a list of responsibilities that seems endless. He shares the love of Christ as he oversees five hospitals and over fifty health centers and dispensaries throughout the entire country.

Dr. Fraley delivers supplies, checks on patients, performs surgery, as well as assists in administration, teaching of the staff and encouraging each facility. His duties require him to spend many days away from home traveling over dirt, rock, and sand roads or paths. He also faces risk traveling among the African tribes and wild animals, which pose life threatening danger at times. In addition, when he travels out into the bush country, he lives as the natives—eating their food, and sometimes sleeping in his vehicle or under the stars.

From 1976-1980, Dr. Fraley and his wife were involved in building a new hospital (located in Kenya) and establishing a school of nursing on one of the largest mission stations of its kind in the world. The hospital provides one of the highest qualities of health care of any mission hospital not only in Kenya but throughout East Africa. The quality of training Dr. Fraley and his staff have developed at the nursing school is as good as any in western civilization. All staff members in this health ministry must profess Jesus as Lord and Savior, and maintain high Christian standards.

Dr. and Mrs. Fraley also assist and work with the Kenyan government in obtaining licenses for many of the long and short-term missionary doctors and nurses coming into the country. He participates with missionaries from different mission organizations in Bible study and prayer groups for their spiritual growth. He is the attending physician for many of the missionaries of all denominations that come into the country, and sat on the Board of Mission for Essential Drugs for over 10 years, an organization he helped establish in order to get medicines at cost for Mission Health Services. He also served as Board Member and Vice Treasurer of the Christian Health Association of Kenya (CHAK) for over 10 years. This organization was developed to serve all of the Protestant Health Services in Kenya consisting of over 260 health units.

The President of Kenya recently asked the health ministries that Dr. Fraley directs, to take over a major health center in a remote area of the country among the poor people there. He agreed to do this, not only to meet the desperate health needs of these people, but it would provide a great opportunity to share the love and salvation of our Lord Jesus Christ. All of the 57 health units under his direction, minister to the poor and needy in remote areas.

His most recent projects include his involvement in the building of a crippled children's hospital and currently the building of a medical training facility and expansion of the nurses training center.

We have barely touched the surface of all that is now happening and has happened for the Lord over the past 25 years on the mission field through the ministry of Dr. Fraley and his wife, as well as others with whom they work. God has blessed them to lead a team of godly and committed Christians to work through in developing these many ministries. All of the glory, praise, and honor, must go to the Lord. As you can see, there is more work to be done than there are hours in a day. Only the power and anointing of the Holy Spirit could give a man, now 68 years old, the strength to accomplish all that has been accomplished.

Dr. Fraley and his wife are among those godly servants who forsook their material possessions, family ties, pleasures, home and country to follow the call of our Lord Jesus—to serve wherever He leads—helping the poor and needy of the world. They are not seen on TV nor do you hear much about them, as they are not in the public eye. They labor selflessly, day in and day out, to share the love and salvation of our Lord Jesus Christ, and reach out to the needs of the sick, hurting, and needy people of this world. Their ministry is built on solid rock. They have stood the test of time in their obedience and faithfulness.

Chapter One
My Testimony

I was raised on a small farm in southwestern Ohio. I grew up in a family of 13 children. I was number 12. My parents were godly people, sincerely dedicated to serving the Lord Jesus Christ. As the 13 children grew up, precept and example trained them. All but one of the 13 have a testimony of their commitment to the Lord Jesus Christ. Many who knew our mother testified that she lived an exemplary Christian life—much like the outstanding women of the Bible as talked about in Proverbs 31.

Growing up, I always had a strong desire to know the Lord. When I was about 7, I joined the church and was baptized in a local creek, thinking this might help me go to Heaven. At age 11, I heard and understood the gospel of Christ for the first time. I came under conviction for three days and nights until I finally made a decision to accept Jesus as Lord and Savior. This was hard for me to do in that I was very shy. I found it very difficult to go forward in church and make a public confession. However, afterwards I tried very hard to live a godly life. I soon found out that my standards were much different than most of my classmates in school, but my commitment was such that this did not bother me.

Upon graduating from high school I entered the Navy. Our country was in the Korean War and I was sure I would be drafted. This was a real time of testing for me in that I found myself to be one of the few committed Christians in the military. Again, the Lord provided an inward strength where this really did not bother me.

While in the Navy, the Lord gave me a great desire to know Him better through His Word. I had a lot of spare time while on ship duty and was able to spend most of those hours in the Word of God. As a normal practice, I would rise two hours before wakeup call to pray, study the Word and memorize Scripture. By the time my four-year tour of duty was over I had memorized over eight hundred verses, word perfect, reviewing about 150 of them every day from morning to night.

It was during my four years of military service that I had a unique—what I would call—supernatural experience that led me to commit my life to the Lord Jesus Christ for His service and direction. The presence of God surrounded me one day as I was reading Hebrews 13:5. The Lord spoke that word to my spirit. It says: *Let your conversation be without covetousness; and be content with such things as you have: for He hath said, I will never leave thee, nor forsake thee* (KJ version). That caused me to commit my life into the Lord's hands for His service and give up my own plans.

After military service, I felt led to enter Bible College in Nyack, New York, being supported by the GI Bill. It was there that I met, Marlene, the girl I would later marry. I learned later that Marlene was committed to becoming a missionary nurse and had plans to serve the Lord in Africa.

A few months after entering Bible College, I was praying one

I started my medical practice in the area where I grew up. My practice grew each year and I was soon earning a net income of $300,000.00 to $400,000.00 per year. I had my own airplane and the nicest Buick one could buy. Our family had a nice home in town. We bought the 100 acre family farm and fixed it up very nicely with tractors, pick-up truck, animals and horses. I was able to buy about everything anyone in the family wanted and it was all paid for.

However, one major thing was wrong spiritually. By setting up my practice here in the states I was out of the Lord's will for my life. I was walking in direct disobedience to the Lord's original call. I had been drawn into *deception* by the enemy and did not know it was happening.

This first *deception* seemed to open the door for me to fall prey to an even greater *deception*. It happened about four years after practicing medicine here in this country. I got involved in a situation, in consideration of others I will not share the details of the situation other than to say that it was definitely sinful, which had the potential of devastating me and destroying everything I had, including my family. I had become blind! I could not see it. Like Eve eating the fruit from the garden, I can also say: *"The enemy deceived me."*

At this point I might digress a little. I think there is an important lesson to be learned for anyone who claims to be a Christian. Although God is very merciful and long suffering, there comes a time when He expects us to clean up our lives and follow the straight and narrow. The sooner the better! Otherwise, He will have to do it for us and we will not like it.

As a physician of many years I have often had to deal with, and attempt to assist Christians with personal problems in their lives, problems that they would not want to share with most other people. This includes pastors and Christian leaders. Often it is the personal problems we have that can amount to secret sins, and they will trip us up in the Christian life. It takes a humble and sincere Christian to admit they have a problem and seek help. This is partly because we are too proud to admit we may have a spiritual problem, or they are of such nature that we just don't want to talk about it.

These problems take the form of lying, cheating, complaining, backbiting, criticizing (especially other Christians, and even more so, those who are anointed for His service), dishonesty (especially in the way we use money), pornography, (which can include TV programs, movies, and now the Internet), masturbation, materialism (excessive affection of things), excessive pleasure, and even fornication, extramarital affairs, homosexuality, adultery, divorce, and on and on. Any of these things, and others that are of the world, can make us insensitive to God's Spirit; therefore, preventing Him from giving us clear direction. That is one reason: *Many are called, but few are chosen.* When God says that we are to come out of the world and be separate, He really means just that and for a good reason which I explain in a later chapter.

I had been *deceived* by the enemy and fell prey to the many attractions and cares of the world. It brought about a major spiritual defeat in my life of disobedience to the Lord and I had not been aware of it. Realizing I was not walking with God after having committed myself to His service, devastated me. From my youth I had had such a strong desire and commitment to serve the Lord. Failing to go to Africa and do the Lord's revealed will literally crushed my heart.

I could not believe I had gotten so far out of the Lord's will. But it happened! I had been active in church during this time. I had studied the Word of God and spent time in prayer, but in my disobedience, I had allowed the enemy to *deceive* me. My actions were beyond the understanding of those who knew me well.

After the veil of my *deception* had been lifted, I began to seek the Lord with all of the strength I had with a true heart of repentance. I sought the Lord for a new filling of the Holy Spirit and the power to walk with Him according to His will as I had once experienced. I put forth every ounce of my being seeking God for *seven* months, studying the Word, meditating, praying and worshiping Him in a state of repentance. I also wanted to know *why so many Christians seemed to be living such defeated lives.*

At the end of this seven-month period, my family and I went on a two-week vacation to Florida. I had decided to spend this time fasting and praying—seeking the Lord—still in a spirit of repentance for my disobedience. I was determined not to stop until I knew beyond a shadow of a doubt that I was filled with the Holy Spirit.

Midway through the second week of our vacation, I awakened one night and knew the presence of the Lord was in the room with me in a special way. Then I began to have visions similar to the one where the Lord had called me to become a doctor. It should be noted that these visions only came when I was living in complete victory and holiness.

The first vision was that of a large head of a beast—very fat looking—hovering over America. It was swallowing up Christians in our country, almost at will. The Spirit of the Lord showed me the meaning of this vision. This beast represented the power of materialism and pleasure in our country. It was swallowing up many Christians by spiritually *deceiving* and overcoming them through the influence of the materialism and pleasure in our society. Those Christians who were being overcome were not aware of what was happening. This is what had first pulled me away and caused my disobedience in not going to the mission field.

The Lord did not give me the full identity of this "beast" that I saw. However, He did convict me that I had been caught up in the system of this beast and had been overcome. It was how I had been deceived and then conquered in my own spiritual walk. It had kept me from obeying the Lord to go to the mission field.

This "beast", working through the powerful temptations of materialism and pleasure, was causing Christians in America to lose their spiritual power. This is why so many have become apathetic toward the deterioration of the biblical standards in our country. It is why so many Christians in America are experiencing major spiritual defeats as thousands of lives and families are being wrought with hurt and suffering.

The enemy is using the system of this "beast" as a powerful tool to attack and destroy America's Christian foundation. It is destroying the biblically based moral standards in our society that have been the guideline the majority of our people have lived by for years. Never before has our spiritual enemy, Satan, been able to attack and change the standards of a society in such a short period of time as he has in America in this last generation.

I am not declaring that the Lord showed me it is wrong to have material things or enjoy good wholesome pleasure. What the Spirit of the Lord did reveal to me through the vision of this "beast" is how the desire for material things in our country, and the exposure to immoral standards through the entertainment industry, have become so strong it is causing Christians to fall prey to *deception*. DECEPTION BRINGS COMPROMISE! Compromise is disobedience to the standards of God's Word. That is how Satan used *deception* to get Eve, then Adam, to sin in the Garden of Eden. I saw that Satan is bombarding our minds, day in and day out, with ungodly and unscriptural ideas and principles using television, radio, and the media as false teachers.

The Lord confirmed to me that this vision I had of a "head of a beast" hovering over America, attacking Christians did come from the Holy Spirit. Following the first vision with four other visions of Jesus Christ is how He quickly did this. Scriptures tell us the Holy Spirit always testifies of Jesus.

The first vision I had of Jesus showed Him giving up His life, willing to pay a tremendous price on the cross, for the salvation of mankind. The following vision showed that Jesus was a very disciplined person, one whom had His face set as a flint. Nothing could deter Him from His call and purpose in life. The third vision of Jesus showed me the great love He has for mankind. That is what it took for Jesus to endure the sacrifice of His life on the cross. The last vision of Jesus showed Him standing at the door of my heart knocking—wanting to come in and re-establish the Lord's will in my life.

These visions had a powerful and profound impact on me. Of course, through these visions the Lord was showing me how He did not deserve the kind of treatment that I had given Him in backing down from my original calling. With all that Jesus had sacrificed for me I had become neglectful, disobedient and unfaithful. I was on a path of "falling away."

21

When I awoke the next morning, I still sensed the presence of the Lord in a very special way. As I got up, the Spirit of the Lord drew me to get my Bible. Almost irresistibly! The vision I had about the "beast" hovering over America was on my mind. I remembered from past Bible studies that there was something written somewhere about a "beast" in the book of Revelation. So, I immediately went to the book of Revelation and began to thumb through its pages. When I came to the **thirteenth** chapter, the Spirit of the Lord seemed to literally take verse 3 off the page of the Bible and sear its full meaning into my mind. I didn't even have a chance to read it. I completely understood the fulfillment of this verse as if I had always known it. Revelation 13:3 reads: *One of the heads of the beast seemed to have had a fatal wound, but the fatal wound had been healed. The whole world was astonished and followed the beast.*

I had never experienced anything like it before. In an instant, I had a perfect understanding of the exact event that fulfilled the wound of the beast in this verse. It was as if I had known it all my life. It was clear as a bell even though the truth is, this was all brand new to me. There was no question in my mind that this had been a supernatural revelation from the Spirit of the Lord.

Before proceeding with my testimony I want to make a statement about what the Spirit of the Lord showed me to be the "wound of the beast." If you are like me, and some others who have heard my story, the revelation given to me that identifies the event that fulfilled the "wound of the beast" in this verse is at first hard to believe. But, I ask that you stay with me. Do not stop here! Please read on and get the rest of the story before you conclude, that is impossible.

What the Lord seared into my mind that fulfilled this prophecy, written nearly 2000 years ago by John about the "wound of the beast," was the event of the surprise attack by the Japanese on Pearl Harbor, December 7, 1941. I will later describe that attack for you in this book. It devastated America's Pacific Naval Fleet and all of our nation's Air Force installations at Pearl Harbor.

Personally, I had several problems with this revelation. Of course it came as quite a shock! My first reaction was, "that is impossible!" You may have the same reaction. A younger person may hardly remember Pearl Harbor. That is why I ask that you read on to at least get the full story. You will, however, have a major advantage over me. You will have the benefit of a tremendous amount of scriptural and historical research that has since been done on the possible truth of this revelation, some of which I summarize in this book.

The reason I immediately had several problems with this revelation was because, over the years, I had been in Bible studies on the book of Revelation. The most common thoughts I had been taught were the book of Revelation was not to take place until some time in the future, that is, from the 4th chapter on. Specifically, until after we were raptured. So I really wasn't too concerned with it. If this revelation was true, the book of Revelation was already taking place and some of it was already history, including this particular verse.

Another shock was; if the "wound of the beast" was the attack on Pearl Harbor that meant this "beast" in Revelation 13 was our own superpower, the United States government. And that was very hard for me to accept. I had always been taught that it would be a particular man who would rise up and rule the world and somehow be associated with the European Economic Community. I never associated the United States as being a major part of this development.

The thought never occurred to me that we have become the greatest superpower in the history of mankind.

However, please do not jump to any false conclusions. There is one thing that I want to make sure is clear. In identifying the United States government as the "beast" superpower of Revelation 13, I am not suggesting that Americans should not love their country, pray for our government leaders, honor the flag, be thankful for living in a free country and more. Quite the contrary! My desire is to preserve our Christian standards and great spiritual history.

I resisted this revelation from the Lord for several days. But the Lord would not let up, or let me have any peace, until I fully accepted the fact that this prophecy about the "wound of the beast" was fulfilled at Pearl Harbor. When I did give in, the Lord anointed me with an overpowering anointing of His Holy Spirit. I seemed to literally vibrate with spiritual power! All I could do was lift up my hands, as if I could actually touch the Lord, and praise the Holy name of Jesus over and over. This special immersion in the power of the Holy Spirit lasted for about six weeks. It served as a confirmation from the Lord that the revelation I had received about the "wound of the beast" and the identification of the "beast" in Revelation 13 was truth.

During this period of time, while the Lord's special anointing was resting on me, I constantly witnessed for the Lord Jesus Christ—seemingly with no effort at all. It just flowed out. And though my words were often no different than at other times when I had witnessed, there was an unbelievable difference in the effect on those people who heard me. Whether I spoke one on one to people or at a church, nearly everyone who listened would come under a heavy conviction of repentance, recommitment, or salvation. Of course, none of this had anything to do with me. It was all the power of the Holy Spirit.

About two weeks after this anointing, or baptism as some would call it, as I was literally immersed in the power of the Holy Spirit—just as real as if I was immersed in water—my younger brother, Bob Fraley, came by for a visit. I was so filled with this revelation I couldn't help but share these things with him. I had no thought of trying to convince him that they were true. I just shared what actually happened. I had no idea that it affected him one way or the other. However, he later shared with me that the Holy Spirit came upon him in a powerful and similar way. He showed him that these things were true, and placed a great desire in his heart to completely serve the Lord Jesus Christ.

Since that time, God has led Bob to do a tremendous amount of study and research to see whether Scripture could support such a revelation. All that I saw in the Spirit at that time has now been confirmed as being in harmony with God's revealed Word. The Bible also states that in the mouth of two witnesses shall a thing be established. Here was another confirmation that this was of the Lord.

After this period of about six weeks, the Lord seemed to lift His special anointing from me. It was then that I came under a period of heavy testing by the enemy. I will not say much about what happened during this time of testing because it was too awful and too scary for me to even talk about. The one comment I will make about this experience is that I know for certain there is a being called Satan, and a place called Hell. It seemed that they unleashed all their powers upon me. I trust that very few people will ever have to experience what I had to go through. However, I did learn that: *Greater is He that is in us, than he that is in the world,* (See 1 John 4:4) and that by trusting in God's Word, we can stand against him (Satan). Since that time, I have walked with a certain "holy fear" that has helped me to stay in the Lord's will and follow His commandments. I count it a great privilege to do so. It actually resulted in serving the Lord in Africa, a very easy and joyful thing to do.

After this time of testing the next thing in line for my wife, and me, was to begin preparations to go to the mission field in Africa. We first went to Tanzania for a year and afterwards to Kenya. We have served the Lord for over twenty-five years in Africa. A short summary of our ministry in Africa is shared at the beginning of this book.

Important Principle to Follow

This revelation occurred in 1971. Since then thousands of hours in research and study of both Scripture and history have been done to test this revelation.

This principle of testing is especially important in my situation because of the way most Christians have been taught on this subject in our country. Without showing how this revelation lines up with Scripture and history, many Christians would reject even the possibility of it being truth.

In the remainder of this book I will share a portion of the scriptural and historical research that has been done on the revelation I received that identifies the "beast" found in Revelation 13. Then I will discuss some of the important principles learned in *knowing the enemy's use of deception,* and *what Christians in America might expect next* from the Lord.

There are many different views taught on the meaning of the symbolic words, which describe the "beast" in Revelation 13. Not once have I ever seen someone state the Lord had revealed to them the exact meaning of a verse that reveals the identity of this "beast." Others have simply offered their personal views.

In fact, hundreds of books have been written about Revelation and this "beast." None of them agree completely with each other, indicating that the full meaning of these Scriptures had just not been revealed. It has always amazed me that when I hear someone teach on this subject they usually give the view that they themselves have been taught and have accepted. They teach it as though it were fact with no room for debate. There is usually no mention of the truth that many godly authors disagree on the exact meaning of many of these Scriptures. Is this the proper and honest way to teach a subject?

Over the past 25 years I have been privileged to serve with fully committed Christians (filled and led by the Holy Spirit) from around the world. I have learned that few of them agree completely as to what the symbolic language in Revelation refers. Most people have their own theories that are based on what they were taught. God obviously has not revealed the full meaning on many areas of the book of Revelation.

Furthermore, having different views in no way affects our salvation or our walk and service to the Lord. The revelation I had is not a new doctrine. You do not need to believe this revelation unless the Holy Spirit and the Word of God that is shared in this book confirms it to you. But, in this time when most committed Christians believe we are near the end of this age, when much of the book of Revelation will come to pass, it cannot hurt you to know that such a revelation that I had <u>did</u> occurr. If God does not confirm it, you can tuck it away in the files of your mind and watch to see what actually takes place as time goes along.

However, the Spiritual teachings that have come from this revelation, which are shared in this book and are backed up by the Word of God, must be taken very seriously. If we are alert and ready and the rapture does occur, no one will complain. But, if we are not alert and ready—have become slothful in our commitment—we could be in for a big surprise. Not only that, you may already be *Caught in the Web of Deception.*

So I encourage you to read on, examine the scriptural backing of this revelation that I received and absorb some of the biblical teachings that are emphasized in this book. If you have become careless in doing the will of God and have been caught up in the world system and its cares, this could change your life and direction. I know it did mine!

There is no greater privilege on this Earth, or in Heaven, than to know and serve our Lord Jesus Christ who loved us and gave His life for us. He paid a tremendous price for our salvation and has every right to expect that we would seriously consider seeking to fulfill the directive given to us in Romans 12:1,2. It reads: *Therefore, I urge you, brothers, in view of God's mercy, to offer your bodies as living sacrifices, holy and pleasing to God—which is your spiritual worship. Do not conform any longer to the pattern of this world, but be transformed by the renewing of your mind. Then you will be able to test and approve what God's will is—his good, pleasing and perfect will.* As this Scripture states, this is only reasonable and makes perfect sense.

Section One

Scriptural Description of the "Beast" Prophesied About in Revelation 13

Chapter Two

Revelation Chapter 13
Verse One

**And I saw a beast coming out of the sea. He had ten horns
and seven heads, with ten crowns on his horns, and on
each head a blasphemous name.**

In the past I had no clue as to the identity of this "beast." Therefore, I always kept right on reading after finishing verse one. John's
use of symbolic language; horns, heads, crowns, etc. seemed too difficult, if not impossible, to decipher. John gives six distinct characteristics in this verse to describe this "beast." They are: (1) "beast," (2)
"coming out of the sea," (3) "ten horns," (4) "seven heads," (5) "ten
crowns on his horns," and (6) "on each head a blasphemous name."

I will examine the research that has been done on each of these
six characteristics. It is hard to find many verses in the Bible that give
such a detailed and exact description as this verse does in describing
this "beast." If the United States government fails to meet the meaning of any one of these descriptive words, then the meaning of the
revelation I received must be questioned.

Description Number One: The word *"beast."*
In finding the meaning of this word, we are fortunate because

the prophet Daniel speaks of "beast" in chapter seven of Daniel, and is told the meaning from an angel (Daniel 7:1-8, 15-17).

The highest authority anyone can use to determine the meaning of a word in Scripture is to use the Bible itself. If the same word is used in other portions of Scripture in the same way, then we need to look at how the word is used and what it means. This is especially a good rule if the Bible is discussing a similar subject. God often reveals His truth through other Scripture. No author writing about a similar topic will contradict another. The Scriptures never fail to be consistent—if an interpretation holds for one passage, it will hold true for another passage. Jesus often referred to another Scripture to give the meaning of what was being said.

In the book of Daniel, the Word of God is clear that the "beasts" Daniel saw referred to powerful governmental authorities—a kingdom, an empire—what we call a superpower.

Daniel used the word "beast" to describe the prophetic vision he had of those superpowers that would affect his people, the Jews. Daniel chapter seven uses this word to describe four great world superpowers: The Babylonian; Media-Persian; Greek; and Roman. In Daniel 7:3 they are called, *four great beasts.* John uses the word "beast" in Revelation 13:1 the same way.

It certainly is in order for Scripture to prophesy about America as we near the end of the Church Age, since we are the greatest superpower ever to exist and our country is the center of Christianity. The United States government is a superpower of the magnitude the angel showed Daniel.

Daniel used the word "beast" when talking about world superpowers in his prophecies and John uses this word in a similar way in

Revelation 13 to simply indicate a dominant world government superpower.

Jesus was born and lived under a government system called a "beast" in Scripture—the Roman government. Likewise the church began under the same governmental system.

The "Beast" Referring to a Man

There are several Bible translations—King James, New International Version and others—that use the pronoun "he," "his," or "him" when referring to the "beast" in Revelation 13. This appears to support the idea that the "beast" in this chapter refers to a man. This concept is often taught in Bible studies. However, that idea runs contrary to the angel's interpretation of what the word "beast" meant in the book of Daniel. It is also contrary to the revelation I received that identified the "wound of the beast." Therefore, more research was done to understand this difference.

It was encouraging to discover there are Bible translations—Revised Standard Version, Philips Translation and others—that <u>do not</u> use the pronoun "he," "his," or "him" to refer to the "beast" in Revelation 13. They use the pronoun "it" or "its." This is consistent with the idea that the word "beast" in this chapter is referring to a government entity not a man. Because of this discrepancy in the various translations, along with the revelation that I had received, it was important to discover which translation is correct. Therefore, help was acquired from a seminary professor who has his doctorate in the Greek language. We wanted to examine the Greek grammar on the use of these two different pronouns: was "he," "his," and "him" correct or was "it," and "its" correct.

The Greek word "*onpiov*" is the <u>noun</u> translated "beast" in Revelation chapter 13. This Greek word in English is the word "*therion.*" The Greek word "*avrov*" is the <u>pronoun</u> throughout Revelation 13 that is used to reference the "beast."

The English pronoun selected to refer to the English noun "beast" must be of the same gender as the noun. A pronoun always carries <u>the same gender</u> as that noun to which it refers. It is the same gender as its antecedent—the noun it replaces. The Greek word used for "beast" in Revelation 13 <u>is neuter gender not masculine</u>. That is critical!

If the original Greek word used for "beast" was <u>masculine gender</u> then "he," "his," and "him" are the appropriate English pronouns to use in translating this chapter. However, the fact the original Greek word for "beast" in this chapter is <u>neuter gender</u> indicates "it" and "its" are the appropriate pronouns to use when translating this pronoun into English. This means John, like Daniel, could definitely be describing the characteristics of a government superpower in these verses, not some man. This is not a hypothetical answer, but a grammatical fact.

Publishers of the Bible agree on this point that the masculine pronoun is not grammatically correct. The King James and New International Version translators have used the wrong pronoun. This is one instance where the incorrect translation has been misleading because it has encouraged the thought that the "beast" in Revelation 13 refers to a man.

Something that has intrigued me since the time of the revelation I received about the wound of the "beast" is that as a physician and surgeon I have been able to bring many people back to life who received a mortal wound. This statement made by John over 1900 years ago, about what seemed to be a fatal wound, has lost a lot of its meaning today through modern medical science if it was referring to a man.

The United States Government fits this **first** descriptive characteristic in verse one of being called a "beast" or world superpower.

Description Number Two: The phrase, *"coming out of the sea."*

This phrase also appears in Daniel. Therefore, its interpretation in Daniel can be used to understand John's use of this phrase in describing the superpower in Revelation 13.

The four beasts that *came up out of the sea* (Daniel 7:3) in Daniel's vision referred to the succession of four great world powers conquering one another, bringing together people from the continents of Africa, Asia, and Europe into a great mixture of customs, cultures, and languages. These superpowers shaped Israel's history from Daniel's day through the last of these four powers, the Roman Empire.

A nation of immigrants, the United States fits this same prophetic description of *coming out of the sea*. America is known as a "Nation of Nations." The peopling of America is one of the greatest dramas in human history. Over the years there has been a massive stream of humanity crossing every ocean and continent to reach the United States representing most of the world's nationalities, races, and religions.

We are the largest cultural-linguistic unit in the world. Yet, we have one primary language, one set of federal laws, and one economy. The melting pot was once a popular image of American assimilation. The largest ethnic strain is of European ancestry, the region of the old Roman Empire, which accounts for about 70.5 % of our people.

Daniel prophesied in chapter 7 that there would be another power, a little one or new country, that would rise up out of the people of the old Roman Empire and that it would become stronger than any of the other powers in its day. This description would certainly apply to us.

The United States Government fits the **second** descriptive characteristic of the "beast" in Revelation 13:1 of *coming out of the sea.*

Description Number Three: The words, *"ten horns."*

Many of the numbers used in Scripture have a symbolic meaning as well as their numerical value. Bible scholars have written entire books presenting a study on the symbolic meaning of numbers and how they are used in Scripture. The number *ten* is used to mean an *all encompassing number.* It represents order. Examples of the number *ten* being used to mean order and all encompassing includes the Ten Commandments, the ten virgins, the ten plagues and so on.

The word *horn* in the Bible is a word that was used to indicate power and authority. If the writer was talking about nations, kingdoms, or countries the word *horns* would represent nations with power, influence, and authority, but *less* power and authority than that of a "beast," or superpower. Daniel used the word *horn* to reference nations and John uses this word in Revelation 13 to mean the same thing.

For Scripture to describe the "beast" in Revelation 13 as having *ten horns* would mean this superpower would have a strong influence over several other nations. It would <u>not</u> necessarily be an exact count of *ten* nations because the symbolic meaning of the word *ten* means, all encompassing, regardless of the number. The Roman Empire, for example, is described in prophetic Scripture as having *ten horns* (see Daniel 7:20 and 24, and Revelation 12:3) yet it ruled over more than 25 other nations.

To use the same meaning of the phrase *ten horns*, in Revelation 13, would indicate this "beast," or government superpower, would also have a strong position of influence over many other countries. These countries would not be superpowers, but regional powers. That is why he refers to them as *horns*.

Examples of this would be countries like Japan and Germany who are economic powers; France and England who are former colonial powers and continue to hold political influence over some countries. Each one of these nations would be called a *horn* in prophetic Scripture, but not a "beast" as we would because they are not superpowers.

The United States is the only country today that can claim to be a superpower. We exercise a certain amount of influence and control over most countries in the world through our economic, military, and political power. When a conflict arises, anywhere in the world, that may affect our well being we usually take some kind of action. It may come through a number of different channels. The action we take is normally done in the name of keeping *peace* which is also a prophetic characteristic given in Scripture about the end-time superpower.

The United States government fits the **third** descriptive characteristic of the "beast" in Revelation 13 of having *ten horns*.

Description Number Four: The words, *"seven heads."*

Seven heads can be understood in a similar way as *ten horns*. Bible scholars have determined that the symbolic meaning of the number *seven* in Scripture represents something being *complete or full*. There are several examples in the Bible. The first that usually comes to our mind is God created the universe in *seven* days. Another one I personally like is found in II Kings chapter five where the military captain, Naaman, was told by Elisha to go and dip himself *seven* times in the Jordan river and he would be healed of his leprosy. The number *seven* is used throughout Scripture to mean the subject being discussed is complete.

The meaning of the word *head* is easier. It simply means *leadership*. To use these two words, *seven heads*, together to describe the "beast" in Revelation 13:1 would mean this government superpower has *complete leadership*. Its leadership is complete in ali areas of world affairs. This superpower would be the leader or number one in commerce, industrial output, output of goods and services, agriculture, military might, political power, economic power, and so on.

We are the only dominant superpower in existence today that is the leader in every area of world affairs. We are the sole superpower with *seven heads*, or complete leadership.

The United States government fits the **fourth** descriptive characteristic of the "beast" in Revelation 13 of having *seven heads*.

Description Number Five: The phrase, *"ten crowns (some translations say ten diadems) on his horns."*

Of all the identifying descriptions that Scripture gives about the "beast" in Revelation 13, this one of having *ten crowns on his horns* is the most unique. It is a very demanding and exact characteristic, therefore, probably the most meaningful. I hope to explain it well enough so you can see what I mean.

The word *crowns*, or as some Bible versions read, *diadems*, was a distinctive mark of royalty among the early Greeks and Romans. The word refers to political position. If a country or nation is being discussed and the word *crown* or *diadem* is used you would know that something was being said about its political position.

When I earlier discussed the phrase *ten horns* we learned from the book of Daniel that the word *horns* in prophecy refers to nations or countries. To add the word *crowns* with the descriptive word *horns* would mean John is making a statement about the political position of these *horns* or nations that the "beast" heavily influences.

What this phrase, *ten crowns on his horns*, means then is that even though this "beast" of Revelation 13 heavily influences other nations in the world, it allows every one of these nations **to politically control themselves.**

How do we know that? Notice where Scripture says the *crown* or political control is located. The *crown* **(political control)** is on the *horn* **(on each nation itself)** not on the *head* **(leadership)** of the "beast." This "beast," or superpower, of Revelation 13:1 does not politically rule or control other countries. It allows each country to have its own ruling government. That is a unique description.

If the "beast" described in Revelation 13:1 politically controlled other countries then Scripture would have used the phrase *ten crowns on his heads* **(the "beast's" political leadership)**. It would not have used the phrase *ten crowns on his horns*.

39

When prophetically describing other superpowers the Bible states the *crowns*, or political control, are on the *heads* of the superpower, not on the *horns*. That is because these other superpowers maintained political control over the countries they heavily influenced rather than allowing each country to politically control themselves. That is how the world powers discussed in Revelation 12:3 and Daniel chapter 7 are described. The crowns are on the *heads* not on the *horns*.

I know of no other superpower in the history of mankind that meets this distinctive characteristic except the United States, not with superpowers! We defeated both Japan and Germany in WW II for example, yet we allowed each country to retain its own political autonomy. We have not tried to rule them politically from Washington.

When you examine the past history of conquering superpowers, they not only politically ruled over the countries they conquered, they usually took all of their goods and used their people for taxes and labor. We have not done that! We have helped rebuild the countries we have conquered.

That is why this particular descriptive characteristic is very unique. It is such a demanding characteristic to meet. No other superpower in the history of mankind has ever met this prophetic description except for our own government.

This imagery of *crowns* and *horns*, of politics and nations, is a telling description of America's relationship with other countries. The United States government maintains more military bases and foreign embassies than any other nation. Our technological, industrial, agricultural, and commercial influence pull even more of the world's peoples into our grasp. Our influence stretches across the globe. Missionaries journeying to the most remote parts of the Earth have found that American brand names, television programs, and popular music have preceded them. But the United States government does not politically rule these countries.

The United States government fits the **fifth** descriptive characteristic of the "beast" in Revelation 13 of having *ten crowns on his horns.*

Description Number Six: The phrase, "*on each head a blasphemous name.*"

Throughout the Old Testament, blasphemy was one of the gravest sins a person could commit. To blaspheme is to make light of the sovereignty of God. In the New Testament, the Greek word used for blasphemy means to injure one's reputation. The Scriptures are very strict in teaching that the holy name of God is extremely sacred. To misuse His name in any way, either in normal conversation or at any time that is not with a sense of awe and majesty, is viewed as blasphemy. It injures and diminishes the true being of God's holiness.

For John to state *on each head a blasphemous name* would mean the leadership of the "beast" in Revelation 13:1 uses the name of God irreverently. That is serious. More so than most of us realize.

Undoubtedly, many of our nation's founding fathers submitted to the Lord's direction. However, in this generation our government began to allow and even promote many evil causes and ungodly standards. Passing out condoms, for example, sanctions promiscuity in schools, which promotes sexual immorality. Prayer was made illegal in school. A law was passed that has allowed the murder of 40 million human lives through abortion. The report card on our society in a recent 30 year period reads: Crime increased 500%; illegitimate births increased 400%; children living in single-parent homes tripled; the teenage suicide rate tripled; the divorce rate doubled; homosexuality began to openly be taught as an acceptable lifestyle; the entertainment industry began to display sexual permissiveness and violence with very little resistance; respect for authority declined dramatically; robbery, murder, hate, greed, violence and other horrors crowd our newspapers everyday that befell unfortunate victims within the past 24 hours.

John's use of the phrase *on each head a blasphemous name* as it applies to the United States would mean that our leaders have allowed and even promote worldly standards while claiming an association with the name of God.

The United States Government fits the **sixth** descriptive characteristic of the "beast" in Revelation 13 of having *on each head a blasphemous name.*

The United States Government <u>fits all six</u> of the characteristics that John gives us to describes the "beast" of Revelation 13:1. If this verse had been written in contemporary English, and the symbols were replaced with their contemporary explanation, it would read something like this:

And I saw a world superpower develop in a new country made up of many nationalities. It influenced many other powerful nations throughout the world; it held a position of leadership in every area of world affairs, although it did not try to politically rule other countries, they were allowed to govern themselves. It used the name of God freely and irreverently in many of its activities.

The following is a quick reference of the words that describe the "beast" in verse one of Revelation 13.

BEAST .... Empire or superpower.

OUT OF THE SEA .... A nation comprised of peoples with diverse cultural and ethnic background.

NUMERAL TEN .... Denotes all encompassing, order, and completeness.

HORNS .... Nations with significant power, authority and influence, but not a superpower.

NUMERAL SEVEN .... Complete or full.

HEADS .... Leadership.

CROWNS OR DIADEM . A distinct mark of royalty or political position.

BLASPHEMY .... To diminish or injure the sacred sovereignty of who God is by misusing His holy name.

Chapter Three

Revelation Chapter 13
Verse Three

One of the heads of the beast seemed to have had a fatal wound, but the fatal wound had been healed. The whole world was astonished and followed the beast.

You will recall the Lord seared the event that fulfilled this prophecy into my mind as though I had known it all my life. It was that clear. It was the event that took place on December 7, 1941 when the Japanese bombed Pearl Harbor.

Four things are stated in Revelation 13:3 about the wound this "beast" received. They are:

1. One of the heads of the "beast" (one area of its leadership) receives what appears to be a fatal wound. One aspect of its superiority is nearly wiped out. An important point about this wound that cannot be over emphasized is the fact that **only** _one_ _of the heads of the beast seemed to have had a fatal wound,_ not all seven. Remember that in verse one of Revelation 13 John said this "beast" had _seven heads_—complete leadership in all areas of worldly influence. We discussed the meaning of this descriptive phrase in chapter two. In verse 3 it is made clear that only one of these seven heads receives what appears to be a fatal wound.

That is exactly what happened to us at Pearl Harbor. It was our military head, or leadership, that received what seemed to be a fatal wound.

2. However, this verse says our wounded head is healed. This aspect of our superpower's leadership recovers.

3. The world is amazed at our recovery. The recovery is dramatic, awesome, and inexplicable. That is exactly what happened in WW II. We won wars on two fronts, the Pacific and European, in about 3-1/2 years. We ended the war with the dropping of the atomic bomb.

4. After the wound heals, the world follows the beast. After WW II many nations aligned themselves with our government and came under our influence. Our recovery catapulted our position of leadership in the world as never before.

Reviewing Military Events

For the American Government to be the "beast" or superpower referred to in Revelation 13, something in our country's past must match the description of a mortal military wound for this prophecy in verse 3 to fit. The question is, what historical event involving the United States military led to the development of our nation becoming the world's greatest superpower?

The event *could not* have occurred within the last generation because we had already become a superpower. And this event must have occurred within the last hundred years because at the time of the Civil War, Americans fought with themselves to decide whether there would be an America. That narrows it down to the wound and its recovery occurring sometime during the first half of the twentieth century.

Both WW I and II were watershed events for the United States. However, World War I saw our foreign policy geared toward our hemisphere. We limited our international influence to Central America and the Caribbean. It was during World War II that we became a power with globe-encircling interests. Our influence in Africa, Asia, Europe, and the Middle East accompanied the Cold War.

Few people today equate Pearl Harbor with this prophecy, a mortal wounding of the United States. It was something horrible that occurred, but not a mortal wound. One of the more common reasons is because when we think of a mortal wound to the "beast" we make the mistake of thinking it applies to all areas of the "beast's" leadership, all seven heads, not just to one area of leadership, <u>one head</u>, as John states in this prophecy.

It is unnerving to see how closely the attack on Pearl Harbor is to John's prophecy, *one of the heads of the beast seemed to have had a fatal wound.* This event definitely describes what seemed to the world to be a fatal wound to our military leadership.

A Brief History of the Attack on Pearl Harbor

Millions of Americans huddled around their radios to hear the news on December 7, 1941. Confusion, shock, and disbelief spread across the nation. The lives of the American people had been thrown into turmoil and fear. America had been attacked for the first time in over a century, and we were at war. It seemed impossible!

Historians, statesmen and journalists throughout the world refer to this attack as one of the greatest turning points in world history. At the time, world leaders viewed this event as a mortal wound to our military leadership. This day of infamy jarred the United States into astonishing activity like no other. It was the catalytic event of the century.

As U.S. soldiers marched off to war, victory gardens sprang up, recycling bins appeared, and gas-rationing cards were used. Factories that produced autos were converted to produce airplanes, boats, and tanks. There was no escape from talk of war. The unthinkable had happened.

The Japanese attack on Pearl Harbor was so sudden, so spectacular, so devastating. It was even more than that—it was one of the turning points in modern world history. So much happened that day— militarily, politically, and psychologically. Many people who lived through the 1900s tend to divide their lives into two periods—before Pearl Harbor and after Pearl Harbor. The U.S. Congress convened a joint committee to investigate the event, and the committee filled forty volumes with its findings.

The duties of men and women in America were changed forever. The Second World War set into motion forces that changed the way Americans work, play, build families, and conduct their lives. The war transformed our land from a provincial, isolationist country to a superpower, a technological hothouse of incredible economic, political, and military power. We shared this superpower role with the Soviet Union until its recent breakup. **Now the United States stands alone.** Never before has one nation achieved such indisputable dominance.

In an effort to find the historical significance of what happened that December morning, it was discovered there is one account that stands head and shoulders above all others: The book, *At Dawn We Slept*, by Gordon W. Prange. It is considered the finest historical work available on the topic of the Japanese attack on Pearl Harbor. Historians and publishers have praised this book as a "masterpiece" and as "authoritative," "unparalleled," "definitive," and "impossible to forget."

Prange was uniquely qualified for the task. He was educated at the University of Iowa and the University of Berlin. Later, he taught history at the University of Maryland. From October 1946 to June 1951, Prange was chief of General Douglas MacArthur's G-2 Historical Section located at General HQ, Far East Command, Tokyo.

From his historical training and firsthand knowledge, Prange knew more about the attack on Pearl Harbor than any other person. He interviewed virtually every surviving Japanese officer who took part in the Pearl Harbor operation, as well as every pertinent source on the U.S. side. His 873-page history of the attack is based on 37 years of research. His work is acclaimed worldwide; it's without equal. It is an invaluable reference. His book was used as a major source of information in making the movie about the attack on Pearl Harbor, "Tora! Tora! Tora!"

Military historians agree that when the Japanese attacked Pearl Harbor the United States suffered the greatest defeat any nation had ever endured at the **beginning** of a war. It is easily one of the most significant naval operations in twentieth-century military history.

During the 1940s and earlier, most Americans believed as did people throughout the industrialized world, that ships represented the ultimate technological achievement. It is difficult to exaggerate the importance of naval power prior to the Nuclear Age. Battleships were the mightiest weapons of war, and luxury liners represented the epitome of western culture. When a great ship sank—*the Lusitania, the Bismarch, and the Titanic*—people listened to the details in horror. They would inspire legends, ballads and movies. Sinking ships were cataclysmic events akin to natural disasters like earthquakes and hurricanes. At Pearl Harbor, the United States had twenty-two ships either sunk or damaged in a matter of hours.

Prelude to the Attack on Pearl Harbor

In the spring of 1940, a large segment of America's Pacific Fleet had been stationed at Pearl Harbor. It was the world's greatest aggregation of warships—a million tons of fighting steel—and it secured the western front of our mighty nation.

United States influence in the Pacific irritated the Japanese. While the European nations fought each other in the 1930s, the island nation of Japan did not want to miss this golden opportunity to build its empire in Southeast Asia. Japan feared that our huge naval program in the Pacific would threaten their ambitious career of conquest.

So, in December 1940, Admiral Isoroku Yamamoto, Commander-in-Chief of Japan's combined fleet, convinced the Japanese Imperial Council to launch a surprise attack against America's Pacific Fleet at Pearl Harbor. He reasoned that if Japan were to achieve political supremacy in the Pacific, it would have to neutralize America's military capacity at Pearl Harbor.

Yamamoto's plan was to catch us sleeping—literally. He knew that just as a weaker judo expert can toss a stronger opponent by catching him off balance, Japan would have to seize the initiative for the island nation to defeat the United States. By striking a fatal blow to the U.S. Pacific Fleet in one bold attack, Yamamoto hoped to gain the military edge in the Pacific for a year. He and his advisors concluded that if Japan had the military advantage for a year they could win a war in the Pacific against the United States.

Yamamoto's plan had merit! The mass majority of the people in America were completely caught off guard. A statement made on February 19, 1941, by Congressman Charles I. Faddis of Pennsylvania can best sum up the United States' perspective prior to the attack on Pearl Harbor. He declared:

> *The Japanese are not going to risk a fight with a first class nation. They are unprepared to do so, and no one knows better than they do. They will not dare to get into a position where they must face the American Navy in open battle. Their Navy is not strong enough and their homeland is too vulnerable.*

It took a year of intense preparation for the Japanese naval forces to be ready. All of the planning had to be done in the strictest secrecy. If the attack did not catch the United States by surprise it would fail. Japanese military planners had several problems to solve before they could launch an attack. To name a few: They had to design and build torpedoes capable of operating in the shallow waters of Pearl Harbor; produce new armor-piercing shells that could be delivered by planes from low altitudes; select and train the pilots for several months on how to fly in and attack an area like Pearl Harbor; the Japanese had to organize a naval task force and teach the personnel how to refuel the ships in the rough northern Pacific Ocean—the route selected to avoid detection to assure a complete surprise. The Pearl Harbor plan was the most highly classified, closely guarded, best-kept secret of World War II.

At 6 o'clock on the morning of November 26, 1941, the Japanese strike force weighed anchor. Twelve days later, just before dawn on December 7, they reached the launching point for their attack: 230 miles due north of the island of Oahu, Hawaii. The Japanese task force of 33 warships, including six aircraft carriers, had successfully sailed on a northern route through rough waters and dense fog to avoid detection by American ships and surveillance aircraft.

Pearl Harbor Day December 7, 1941

The attack came with startling swiftness that Sunday morning. On every Japanese carrier, the scene was the same. The engines sputtered to life, up fluttered the signal flag, then down again, and one by one, their aircraft roared down the flight decks drowning the cheers and yells from the crews. Plane after plane rose in the sky, flashing in the early morning sun that peeked over the horizon. This airborne armada consisted of 353 planes. It represented the largest concentration of air power in the history of warfare. On the island of Oahu, American sailors were unaware of the tremendous fighting force that would send many of them to a watery grave.

Perfect timing was essential. The Japanese knew full well that if anything went wrong, the entire surprise attack would collapse. They were dead on course. Their mission: destruction of the U.S. Pacific Fleet at Pearl Harbor and all of the nearby American Air Force installations.

It was 7:40 AM when the first Japanese pilots sighted Oahu's coastline—still undetected. The element of surprise belonged to the Japanese. As the first wave of planes approached Pearl Harbor they deployed into three groups. They first struck our Air Force bases so our fighter planes could not get airborne to counterattack their bombing of Pearl Harbor. They hit Hickam Air Force Base, Wheeler Field, Bellows Field, Kaneohe Naval Base and the Naval Air Station at Ford Island.

Japanese pilots, operating from six aircraft carriers, flew in at treetop level bringing massive destruction to our air bases. Hangars were burned, barracks were razed, and hundreds of men were killed. A total of 341 U.S. planes were destroyed or damaged on the ground that Sunday morning. Since all of the air bases were so close, the attacks all came at the same time. Everything happened at once.

But the assault on the airfields was only the beginning of the Pearl Harbor drama. Inside the harbor were 96 warships of the United States Pacific Fleet. Included were 8 cruisers, 29 destroyers, 5 submarines, assorted mine craft and 8 U.S. battleships: the USS *West Virginia*, USS *Arizona*, USS *Oklahoma*, USS *Nevada*, the *Tennessee*, the *Pennsylvania*, the *California* and USS *Maryland*.

At approximately 8:10 AM the battleship USS *Arizona* exploded, having been hit by a 1,760-pound armor-piercing bomb that slammed through her deck and ignited the main fuel tank. In less than nine minutes, she sank with 1,177 of her crew, a total loss. The USS *Oklahoma*, hit by several torpedoes, rolled completely over, trapping over 400 men inside. The *California* and *West Virginia* sank at their moorings, while the *Utah*, converted to a training ship, capsized with more than 50 of her crew. The *Maryland*, *Pennsylvania*, and *Tennessee*, all suffered significant damage. The *Nevada* attempted to run out to sea but took several hits and had to be beached to avoid sinking and blocking the harbor entrance.

As the Japanese dive-bombers rocked the harbor, the mammoth gray ships along Battleship Row, writhing from the explosions of bombs and torpedoes, burned at their moorings, sending billows of black smoke into the morning skies over the island of Oahu. The Japanese dealt crippling blows to ship after ship. Most of the damage was done in the first fifteen minutes. Mitsuo Fuchida, the Japanese commander who led the first formation of planes, later wrote: *The harbor was still asleep in the morning mist.*

The attack on Pearl Harbor ended at about 9:45 AM. In less that two hours the Japanese had immobilized most of our air strength at Oahu, and nearly eliminated their chief objective, the U.S. Pacific Fleet. The once-mighty U.S. military fortress at Oahu had been pulverized. As the drone of enemy formations disappeared over the horizon heading back to their carriers, they left behind a scene of horrible chaos—crackling flames, moaning men, and hissing steam. Half-submerged ships were strewn about the harbor, tilting at crazy angles. Wreckage floated across the oily surface of the water as bodies washed ashore.

As the billows of black smoke over Oahu began to clear, United States forces assessed the damage. Twenty-two ships, including *eight battleships,* were sunk or heavily damaged and more than *340 American aircraft* had been destroyed. Japanese losses totaled 29 aircraft destroyed and 74 damaged.

The Japanese operation at Pearl Harbor was a stroke of military genius incomparable to any other in the history of warfare. The

Japanese secured mastery of the Far East in a couple of hours. In Germany, news of the defeat tempted Hitler to declare war on the United States.

The Fatal Wound is Healed

The event that December morning was more than a stunning military operation. The attack energized the fighting spirit of Americans as nothing else could. The United States jumped to its feet, despite the wound that had cut the heart out of its military, to present the most fearsome warrior the world had ever known.

During the next three and a half years, the United States forged a war machine that conquered enemy forces in European and Asian theaters. It transformed the United States from a provincial, regional power to a technological, military, and political titan stretching across both hemispheres and changed forever the American way of life.

World War II left the nations of Europe and the Pacific Rim in shambles. Many people not only lost their homes, they lost their means of livelihood as well. The fighting destroyed factories, businesses, power plants, roads, bridges, rail lines and much more. Germany, England, Japan, and many other nations lost their industrial capacity. The infrastructure needed for economic productivity had been wiped out by the war.

These nations also lost a whole generation of industrial and government managers during the war—the leadership necessary for business enterprise. Consequently, the economic strength of these nations experienced a severe setback. England's financial and political power, for example, never really returned to the previous status quo. It went from being an industrial power with globe-encircling interests to a more internally focused nation with a moderate role in today's international affairs.

While the European and Pacific powers crawled out from under the rubble of World War II, the United States was on its way to economic supremacy. World War II actually enhanced America's economic position.

None of the fighting had occurred on American soil, so we emerged as the only major world power with its industrial and agricultural output intact. This brought the development of a lifestyle for the people in our country that was unheard of before the war.

Production within American factories after the war continued at a steady clip as we were in a unique position to furnish our wartime allies and enemies with many of the products and services the people in those countries needed. This allowed the average United States worker to have a steady job with a good income. Few of those in the industrial world could boast higher pay, more extensive fringe benefits, or better working conditions.

During the next 30 years after World War II, American products achieved worldwide reputation. We were the "great society" emerging. American companies captured first place in the production of automobiles, machine tools, electronic equipment, and many other vital industries. The output of our land with rich quality agricultural goods was unsurpassed.

We provided the major share of the goods and services needed around the world in the generation that followed World War II. This created an impressive trade surplus. Year after year following the war, Americans sold far more overseas than they bought, and billions of excess dollars from around the world poured into the U.S. economy.

As a result, the American standard of living shot up beyond previous imagination. The average American family claimed vast worldly possessions that were unprecedented in the history of mankind. With less that 7% of the world's population, we accumulated half of the world's wealth and consumed a full third of the world's resources each year. From a material standpoint, Americans lived better than virtually all people throughout the world.

After World War II the American lifestyle became the envy of people everywhere as Americans routinely enjoyed products and services completely out of reach for people in other lands. Those categorized as poor in America would have been in the upper class in many countries. Our country emerged as the greatest political, military, industrial, and economic power ever to exist on the face of the Earth. We, indeed, had received the throne of the world as John prophesied the "beast" would receive in Revelation 13:2. This was soon proven as many countries aligned themselves with the United States Government. The entire world was awestruck by the way the United States demonstrated its great power and ended the war with the dropping of the atomic bomb. *The fatal wound had been healed,* as stated by John in Revelation 13:3.

It is important to note, that I am not saying there was anything wrong with the way our economy flourished after World War II. I cannot pass judgment on that. I have given you a brief review of our economic history, because it relates to the development of a materialistic lifestyle attitude that John warned about in Revelation 13, and Jesus warned about when referring to our day. Their prophetic warnings of *spiritual deception* are later discussed in detail.

Remembering Pearl Harbor

Former President George Bush journeyed to Hawaii December 7, 1991, to revisit Pearl Harbor on the 50th Anniversary of the Japanese attack. The years have slipped by quickly, and most Americans have all but forgotten the scars of the attack on Pearl Harbor. However, the stark horror and grim reminder of defeat that Sunday morning which caught our country in the fierce vortex of history will live forever through the Arizona Memorial, dedicated on Memorial Day, 1962.

USS Arizona[1]

A single 1760-pound armor-piercing action bomb sank the battleship Arizona. The bomb penetrated through six decks of steel and exploded in the main aviation fuel tank. A tremendous internal chain reaction followed. The force of the explosion was so great it raised the bow of the ship completely out of the water, and split her right behind the number one gun turret. The Arizona sank in less than nine minutes. Out of her crew of 1,543 men, 1,177 lost their lives in those few awful minutes.

Arizona Memorial Spans Sunken USS Arizona[1]

Today, the *USS Arizona* rests peacefully in an upright position under 38 feet of water at the bottom of Pearl Harbor. Oil still rises from her rusting hull and the 1100 men still entombed there mirror the most eloquent witness to the fury of defeat on Pearl Harbor Day.

Arizona Memorial Design Theme[1]

It was astounding to discover the theme used for building this memorial reflects the prophecy given by John in Revelation 13:3 when he said: *One of the heads of the beast seemed to have had a fatal wound, but the fatal wound had been healed.* This memorial was structurally designed with a sag in the middle to express our initial defeat—a wound to our military—but stands strong at the ends to express our recovery and victory—the wound was healed.

Other Verses

An analysis of other verses in Revelation 13 and Daniel 7 have also been completed. They too confirm the identity of the "beast" in Revelation 13. However, I have chosen not to linger on this issue. The research I have shared in detail about verse one and verse three is more than sufficient for you to see the possibility that Scripture supports the revelation I received. These two verses are the most descriptive and difficult to meet. In the balance of the book it is more important that I direct my attention to **the significance of this revelation** to the body of Christ.

---

[1]Photographs of the USS Arizona and the USS Arizona Memorial are assumed to be in the public domain. These images were reproduced for educational purposes. An unsuccessful attempt was made by the author to discover the identity of the photographer in order to credit them for their work.

Section Two

Satan's Use of Deception

Chapter Four

Spiritual Deception

He (the beast) **was given power to make war against**
the saints and to conquer (overcome) **them**
(Revelation 13:7).

The word *conquer* in this verse brings to mind the defeat of one
army by another. This is, in fact, a good illustration because the word
means to overcome, defeat, or subdue, not obliterate or eliminate.
John is prophesying that the American society will have the power to
overcome Christians and keep us from walking in the power of the
Holy Spirit, the power source that is necessary for us to live the normal victorious Christian life.

Dr. Billy Graham has said that, according to his research, at least
90 percent of all Christians in America are living defeated spiritual
lives. Others who are in a position to know the spiritual pulse of
America have made similar statements.

Any American willing to face reality must admit that spiritually
we are in serious trouble. Soon after WW II the moral standards that
bound our nation and our people together for centuries began to
unravel. What was unthinkable a generation ago has now become
commonplace in our society.

Not only have the moral standards of our society deteriorated drastically, so have the standards of Christians. Christians have become more tolerant and indifferent to many of the sins described in the Bible that are now flaunted in our culture. The result is while we say we are standing against the tide, in reality we are simply a few decades behind the world's acceptance of 'new' moral standards. Therefore, what was permissible by worldly standards in American society 20-30 years ago is now largely acceptable to Christians. Finding a Christian who has a *fear of sinning* is rare these days rather than the norm as it was in days gone by.

The character of the average Christian in America has changed. We have allowed society to exchange our commitment to righteousness for a spirit of tolerance towards the ways of the world. We need to look no further than ourselves to find the real reason behind the corruption and violence in our nation, and the heavy toll it has taken on the American people.

Christians in America have lost their spiritual discernment. Many do not recognize that they live in the middle of a spiritual war zone and are being hit daily in every way imaginable to bend and compromise biblical standards. In America, Christians no longer have to go out into the world to make contact with it. Through the power of the electronic media, and just about everything else taking place in our society, the world's influence searches us out.

The Christian family has never felt the power and pull of a worldly society as we must contend with today. There is a spiritual battle taking place and it is destroying the biblical standards that the majority of Americans once honored and lived by. No one, regardless of how hard they may try, can avoid the spiritual conflicts we are experiencing from the influence of our society. It is impossible! They are too strong.

Christians are losing many of the battles coming from the influence of our society just as John prophesied in Revelation 13:7. Hundreds of thousands of Christians in America have been hurt in the process of the warfare currently being raged by our enemy. Families have been devastated and many lives have been afflicted with hurt and pain. Christian leaders and church members alike have fallen into sin, especially sexual sins and the breaking up of marriages! It appears to be happening at an accelerated pace all over the country.

The majority of Christians in America are not prepared to stand against the spiritual battles taking place to control the hearts and minds of the American people. I was a victim! I experienced the attacks of the enemy from the "beast" system first hand. People who knew me in my youth, through the Navy, and in my college days would tell you I was a very dedicated Christian. I had a very close walk with the Lord. I had committed my life to be used in service for only Him. But the power of the "beast" system overcame me. It *deceived* me and I fell. Only by the grace of God was my deception lifted. Then through repentance, prayer, and spending a lot of time in the Word of God, I was fully restored. Not that my family and I haven't suffered consequences from my defeat, because we have. But it will soon be 30 years ago that the ministry of my wife and I began and it has been greatly blessed by the Lord. We have been able to meet the needs of many poor and suffering people in Africa.

Warfare

Spiritually, *deception* is a terrible thing. I certainly am not qualified to cover this subject as thoroughly as others. But I am compelled to share some insights hoping it might help other Christians.

The Bible teaches that Satan attacks God's people in two different ways in spiritual warfare: *persecution and deception.* Scripture and history record many examples of both. In the last days however, the Bible warns that Satan's primary attack against the central area of Christianity will first be *deception.*

There is no question that America has been God's chosen land for the center of Christianity in these last days. There is a church located every few blocks in most towns across this nation. Teaching from the Bible can be heard day and night on radio and television. The Bible is the number one bestseller. Millions of books with a Christian message are sold each year; religious publishing has become a major business. Christian missionary organizations are spending millions of dollars to take the gospel of Jesus Christ throughout the world.

Our spiritual history reveals the discovery of America and our early development were delayed until just the right time. It was soon after the Word of God was made available to the public and the period of the Dark Ages was over. America has a special calling by God. America has had the funds and resources to spread the Word of God throughout the world in these, the last days.

But don't think for a moment that the enemy is going to be idle. As we grow in the Lord, what we learn from the Word and our experience is that anything of God involves great spiritual battles. Satan's tactics are ruthless and deadly. "He always plays hardball." The way God has developed our nation's spiritual history, one should expect that we would be in for some fierce spiritual battles. Prophetic Scripture brings to light the method and means that Satan is using here in America to try and defeat the spiritual base which God has established in our land for these last days. *That is the theme of this book.*

Since God created Adam and Eve, God has had an Enemy called, Satan. Satan has always developed a scheme alongside any spiritual development of God, to counter-attack, undermine, and try to destroy God's purpose. He is an enemy who in the past caused Adam and Eve to fall. He caused lawlessness and wickedness to become so terrible, God had no choice but to cleanse the Earth by a flood. He developed the spirit of rebellion and permissiveness so strongly in God's chosen race, Israel, they turned against the ways of God.

In the first 300 years of the church, Satan's attacks against Christians, working through the Roman government, were so harsh an estimated three million Christians were persecuted for their faith. They were hunted down like animals and put to death by every cruel torture man could devise. They were torn to pieces, thrown to wild animals, beheaded, burned, crucified and buried alive.

Satan's attacks became so severe on the church during the Dark and Middle Ages, God prepared a place of near obscurity to protect it and His Word. The church had to operate primarily through the underground during this period of time.

After Martin Luther and the Reformation, Satan continued his attacks against Christians during the Reformation Wars. In country after country, nation after nation, Christians were brutally massacred. They were thrown into dungeons, scourged, tortured on the rack and burned at the stake.

In the Netherlands over 100,000 Christians were slaughtered between the years 1566 and 1598. On August 24, 1572, in France, 70,000 Christians were massacred at one time in what has become known in history as St. Bartholomew's Massacre.

By the year 1600, in Bohemia, nearly 80% of a population of four million people were Christians. Historians report nearly 3,200,000 (all of the Christians) were exterminated by a crusade.

In Spain, the effects of the famous Spanish Inquisition left over 100,000 dead and a reported 1,500,000 were banished from the country.

By 1700 the major thrust of restoring biblical Christianity had moved across the sea to a land called America—a land it seems, that the Lord kept from being explored until after the Reformation.

As we near the day of our Lord's return, God's enemy is hard at work. He has launched an all out attack on our homeland. But as was often the case with God's people in the Old Testament, Satan's warfare in America is being carried out in a different way. He is using a different method in America because many of the laws by which our country was founded were based upon biblical principles. This has limited his use of persecution. Therefore, most of his strategy has been through the use of *deception*. *Deception* can be an insidious and dangerous weapon that is very shrewd and often goes undetected.

Many Christians **have not** been properly taught to guard against the enemy's powerful influences coming from our society. This has caused scores of lives and homes—Christian homes—to suffer a lot of pain. Pastors and Christian counselors are flooded with requests to counsel emotionally hurting Christians. Many are having the same family and personal problems as the people of the world. That should not be!

Every American should be thankful to live in a land that God chose to be His home base to take the Gospel of Jesus Christ through-out the world during this time called the last days. But this does require that we understand and be well prepared for the spiritual battles that we can expect from God's enemy. So far the enemy is winning! He is destroying the biblical standards in America as our spiritual defeats increase. We appear blind as to what *deception* really means, therefore, go about living our lives unprotected which allows the "beast" system to overcome Christians almost at its will.

Deception centers on motivating Christians to step out independent of God's Word, primarily for the purpose of satisfying, serving or pleasing our **self life**. We can expect Satan's use of *deception* to increase and become more severe.

Satan's First Attack Was Through Deception

The fall of Adam and Eve helps us understand how Satan uses *deception* against God's people. As their story begins to unfold in the book of Genesis, we notice that at first everything was good. There is no sign or hint of rebellion. *God saw all that He had made, and it was very good. And there was evening, and there was morning—the sixth day* (Genesis 1:31).

There was no opposition present. It was a lovely picture of fellowship between God and His creatures, with God providing the perfect setting for man. God and man walked together in happy communion. The Bible presents this scene as a blessed picture of love and peace.

God's word to Adam and Eve at that time to obey and express their love was short and simple. *The Lord God took the man and put him in the Garden of Eden to work it and take care of it. And the Lord God commanded the man, "You are free to eat from any tree in the garden;*

71

but you must not eat from the tree of the knowledge of good and evil, for when you eat of it you will surely die" (Genesis 2:15-17). Just one command to keep! You would not think that would be difficult.

The method Satan used to cause Adam and Eve to fall from keeping this command was *deception*. The temptations and choices we make every day are displayed for us in this tragic story. Satan has not changed his method of attack for the child of God. He has used the same basic pattern throughout history.

There was a sweet fellowship existing in the Garden of Eden. Satan knew if he could only cause Adam and Eve to step out and become independent of this one command, not to eat from the tree of the knowledge of good and evil, it would break the bonds of that fellowship and God would lose something which was most precious to Him. Satan cared nothing for the suffering that would follow. This has been his objective throughout the history of Israel and the church, and it is still his objective today.

Satan employed several tactics and temptations to accomplish his goal in the Garden of Eden. He would love to remove the third chapter of Genesis from the Bible, for here we see his plan of *deception* that he used in the garden. His methods are still the same to this day for the child of God.

> *Now the serpent (the animal Satan spoke through) was more crafty than any of the wild animals the Lord God had made. He said to the woman, "Did God really say, 'You must not eat from any tree in the Garden'?"*
>
> *The woman said to the serpent, "We may eat fruit from the*

trees in the garden, but God did say, 'You must not eat from the tree that is in the middle of the garden, and you must not touch it, or you will die.'"

"You will not surely die," the serpent said to the woman. "For God knows that when you eat of it your eyes will be opened, and you will be like God, knowing good and evil."

When the woman saw that the fruit of the tree was good for food and pleasing to the eye, and was also desirable for gaining wisdom, she took some and ate it. She also gave some to her husband, who was with her, and he ate it (Genesis 3:1-6).

Satan's technique to bring *deception* into the heart and mind of Adam and Eve is described in these verses.

<u>Satan's **first** attack technique was to implant thoughts of doubt and then, if not dealt with, outright denial of the meaning of God's word (Genesis 3:1-4).</u>

Daily, hourly, we are confronted with spiritual issues in our everyday lives that challenge the standards of God that are given in Scripture. Count on the enemy to raise doubts in your mind concerning the meaning and importance of following God's Word. He implants his doubts through our subconscious, through the many teaching avenues of the world's electronic media such as television, movies, the Internet, through books and magazines, friends and any other way available to him through the world system.

If we are not careful, and stay alert, we will begin to reason in our own mind, just like Eve. If we do, there will be a strong temptation to serve our own desires, to serve **ourselves**, rather than to be obedient to the standards of God. Our subconscious will play tricks on us. We begin to think: *It really won't make any difference to God, or God's Word really doesn't mean that, does it?* If we allow this process to take hold of our heart and mind Satan's next step will be to cause the doubt to become an outright denial. *No, God understands, He doesn't mind. He wants me to have what I think is best for me.* If we accept that position, we will ignore God's Word, as Adam and Eve did, which breaks our communion with God and can cause us to suffer a spiritual defeat by falling into *deception.*

Satan's **second** attack technique was to deceive Adam and Eve to elevate themselves, *to be like God,* so that they made their own decisions about right and wrong (see Genesis 3:5).

Satan deceived Eve to rebel against God's spoken Word by tempting her to be independent and use human wisdom and reasoning to decide right and wrong, "knowing good and evil." God did not equip humans with the knowledge of good and evil. If we do not follow the Word of God our standards will usually be established by the standards of the society in which we live.

When Christians become independent and attempt to reason and decide "right and wrong" on our own, apart from God's Word, we can be sure Satan will be right there. He will lure us into rebelling against the standards found in God's Word, in favor of our own **self** interest to serve our desires, just as he did Eve.

When Satan attacks Christians through *deception* he tempts the desires of our flesh—those things that serve the self-life. It could be any number of things; beauty, material possessions, knowledge, wisdom, immoral thoughts, sex, lust, pride, position, power, things of pleasure, and others. If successful, Satan will cause us to suffer spiritual defeats. It is much different than when he attacks Christians through *persecution*, which causes physical harm.

> *When the woman (Eve) saw that the fruit of the tree was good for food (lust of the flesh) and pleasing to the eye (lust of the eyes), and also desirable for gaining wisdom (pride of life), she took some and ate it (Genesis 3:6).*

When the Lord saw what Eve had done, He said to her, ..."*What is this you have done?*" *The woman said, "The serpent deceived me, and I ate*" (Genesis 3:13).

Another important point to learn from Satan's attack on Adam and Eve is how freely he used the name of God. That is one of his major traps when attacking God's children through *deception* for self-serving interests. He didn't ask Eve to deny God or to quit walking with God. He knew it was important to her to follow God. He just encouraged her to step out and disregard God's Word. He caused her to doubt that God was really serious about the one command He had given them. ...'*You must not eat fruit from the tree that is in the middle of the garden, and you must not touch it, or you will die*' (Genesis 3:2).

The use of *deception* is also graphically illustrated when Satan tried to trap and deceive Jesus. Satan did not tempt Jesus with the obvious vices of the world. He didn't tempt Him to deny God or to quit being religious. He tempted Jesus with self-serving attractions, just as he had tempted Eve. He wanted Jesus to step out on His own to become independent and make His own decisions, rather than to follow the principles of God's Word.

Satan tempted Jesus to serve the **self-life**. The **first** temptation was with *the lust of the flesh.*

Then Jesus was led by the Spirit into the desert to be tempted by the devil. After fasting forty days and forty nights, he was hungry. The tempter came to him and said, "If you are the Son of God, tell these stones to become bread." Jesus answered, "It is written: 'Man does not live on bread alone, but on every word that comes from the mouth of God'" (Matthew 4:1-4).

God was not going to deprive Jesus of food, but it was to be provided according to God's timing and will, not Satan's. Jesus knew He was not to perform a miracle to serve His own self-desires, even if it would help prove who He was. The **second** temptation was *the pride of life.*

Then the devil took him to the holy city and had him stand on the highest point of the temple. "If you are the Son of God," he said, "throw yourself down. For it is written: '"He will command his angels concerning you, and they will lift you up in their hands, so that you will not strike your foot against a stone."' Jesus answered him, "It is also written: 'Do not put the Lord your God to the test'"(Matthew 4:5,6).

This time Satan tempted Jesus to be proud of the fact He was a child of God by trying to get Him to perform a miracle to serve His own self-interest. He tempted Him to do a foolish thing to prove God would save Him. Jesus again responded to the temptation by quoting Scripture. The **third** temptation was *the lust of the eyes.*

The devil led him up to a high place and showed him in an instant all the kingdoms of the world. And he said to him, "I will give you all their authority and splendor, for it has been given to me, and I can give it to anyone I want to. So if you worship me, it will all be yours." Jesus answered, "It is written: 'Worship the Lord your God and serve Him only'" (Luke 4:5-8).

What a heavy temptation—to be offered all the authority and splendor of the things of the world! We have difficulty in not bowing to this temptation when offered far less than what was shown to Jesus. Again, notice that Satan tempted Jesus' self-life—something that would serve His personal being.

When attacking through *deception*, all of Satan's temptations are directed toward serving or doing something for our **self** though we may not recognize it. He may even use what appears to be a godly cause. But, if the inner motivation is to serve the desires of our flesh or promote something for our ego, **be on guard**.

Another good example of Satan tempting Jesus came through a friend. It is found in Matthew 16. Jesus had asked His disciples the question, *"But what about you?" he asked. "Who do you say I am?"* Simon Peter answered, *"You are the Christ, the Son of the living God."* Jesus replied, *"... this was not revealed to you by man, but by my Father in heaven"* (Matthew 16:15-17). Peter had received a revelation from God. Notice what happened immediately following this revelation.

From that time on Jesus began to explain to His disciples that He must go to Jerusalem and suffer many things at the hands of the elders, chief priests and teachers of the law, and that he must be killed and on the third day be raised to life. Peter took him aside and began to rebuke him, "Never, Lord!" he said. "This shall never happen to you!" Jesus turned and said to Peter, "Out of my sight, Satan! You are a stumbling block to me; you do not have in mind the things of God, but the things of men" (Matthew 16:21-23).

Peter receives a revelation from God. Then in the very next scene he states the desire of Satan. Why? The motivating force was self-preservation for Jesus over and above the will of God. This time Satan tempted Jesus through someone He loved to seek for self-interest. Jesus knew the will of God and, therefore, let Peter know that his thoughts of self-preservation on this occasion were from the enemy.

Knowing the various ways in which our enemy attacks us through *deception* is important to understand in these last days. The Scriptures warn us *deception* will be a primary method Satan will use to attack Christians in the end-times. The moral fruits produced by our society in this generation prove this to be true. Paul wrote: *The Spirit clearly says that in later times some will abandon the faith and follow deceiving spirits…* (I Timothy 4:1).

A definition of deceiving spirits would be: *Seducing or deceiving spirits tempt God's people to trade the truth of God's Word to accept something that is contrary to the Word of God. They try to make something wrong seem innocent. To perform their acts of seduction they attempt to make their enticements irresistible. They try to make the difference between black and white seem like a shade of gray. If we do not know the Word of God and diligently seek righteousness, and hate every evil way, then we will become susceptible to deceiving spirits, for this is one of the greatest dangers in the last days.*

At various times we have all fallen victim to *deception* in one way or another in our Christian walk. It has caused a multitude of personal problems, pressures and conflicts for Christians and requires that we understand another important biblical principle. It is that of repentance and confession. Without it our position of living in victory through the power of the Holy Spirit is seriously affected.

Deception by Satan is difficult to discern in these days because he has so many weapons at his disposal. That is why we need all the insight we can gain on this subject. The Bible says: *The heart is deceitful above all things and beyond cure. Who can understand it?* (Jeremiah 17:9).

A Story of Deception

The following story of an eagle helps to see the techniques used to develop *deception*. Maybe it will be meaningful and helpful to you in your understanding. I do not know the original author of this story.

The eagle is an amazing specimen of God's creation. It is mentioned over 30 times in Scripture. Eagles are swift, clocked at 120 to 150 miles per hour in flight. Their powerful seven-foot wing span allows them to soar and glide effortlessly at heights up to one-half mile, and the aerodynamics of their wing construction permits flight in winds of hurricane force.

The eagle's eye has two fovea (areas of acute vision) which gives them the ability to spot a rabbit two miles away. Their great depth perception allows them to dive at speeds up to 200 miles per hour. They have 270-degree peripheral vision. Their two sets of eyelids permits closing one, which is clear, and protects the eyes from dust and wind during flight.

The eagle's decisive appearance is different from other birds, due to a bony protrusion, which extends outward over the eyelid, and is not found in most other fowl. A stern and decisive appearance, along with its other unique characteristics, gives the eagle a royal pose. Its grandeur and grace have been revered and esteemed for centuries. The eagle has been chosen as the official symbol of some of the greatest countries and leaders including the Romans, Charlemagne, Napoleon and America.

Picture in your mind this monarch of the sky perched high on a mountain ledge overlooking a valley below with a beautiful stream, trees and mountains in the background. This majestic eagle you have envisioned has a clear view of the entire area below him as he sits basking in the morning sun.

After bathing in the sun for awhile, enjoying his domain on this particular morning, the eagle launched himself into the air. He sailed over the green valley and swooped down toward the stream, heading for his favorite fishing spot to catch his breakfast.

When he arrived at the stream's bank his keen eyes noticed there was a slight change near the area where he normally fished. There, near the shore, close to his fishing spot, was a large rock, about two to three feet in diameter and two feet high. It was something new. The eagle knew this rock had never been there before. Therefore, to him it appeared dangerous.

The eagle flew right on by his fishing spot this morning without stopping and sailed to a nearby tree. He perched on a limb so he could observe the area. He wanted to determine if this new and strange object might be harmful. He sat there for better than an hour, his keen eyes looking up and down the stream. In time he could tell there was no activity around; he saw no danger, so he sailed down and landed on the rock.

Next to the rock about 10-15 feet away from the stream, in the nearby grass, was a large, beautiful fish. Fish are one of an eagle's favorite foods. He was quickly drawn to the fish, but he was puzzled. If the fish had been on the shore near the stream, he thought, that would have been normal. But there it was in the grass, several feet from the shore, and that seemed out of order to him.

The eagle sat there for awhile. He was suspicious. Things didn't seem right. His sharp eyes scanned every grassy area around, all the nearby bushes, and the shore of the mountain stream. There seemed to be no danger.

He jumped off the rock, clutched the fish in his claws and was about to fly away when he noticed another fish lying nearby in the grass. Then he saw another! There were three or four beautiful, plump fish. The wilderness was caring for his needs this morning in a most amazing way!

On the other side of the stream, however, a wise trapper hiding in a thick clump of bushes watched every move the eagle made. This trapper had been promised a large sum of money to capture an eagle alive. And he knew the wise eagle would require him to use his best and most crafty skills.

The eagle ate well that day. The next day, after his morning sunbath, he returned to his favorite fishing spot. The rock was still there. He sailed to the nearby tree to observe the area—this time for only a few minutes. This morning it did not take as long for him to be satisfied there was no danger.

The eagle flew to the rock and after landing, found the supply of fish had been miraculously renewed. This was unbelievable! Mother Nature was surely providing for him in a beautiful way. This would give him more time to sit on his perch and soar through the heavens, viewing his lovely mountain and valley domain.

After several days had passed, the eagle found that each morning the supply of fish had been replenished. He was becoming conditioned. Now each morning he would fly directly to the rock. After landing, he would jump down, grab a fish, jump back on the rock and sit there to eat and enjoy his breakfast. When finished, he would jump down, clutch another fish in his claws and fly off, taking the second fish to his nest high on a cliff for a meal later in the day. The eagle loved it! This was saving him better than half of every day, which he could use for soaring through the sky and perching high in the cliffs, two of his favorite pastimes.

After the eagle had developed a frame of mind of acceptance the trapper was ready for his next move. He made a strong hoop like a fish net about four feet in diameter. He attached to the hoop a long handle with a curved bow. The next night he went to the mountain stream where he had placed the rock and carefully dug the long handle into the ground, positioning it at an angle. The hoop hovered about three feet above the rock, yet the bow in the handle kept the net fairly level over the rock. Then, as he had been doing every night, he spread fish out in the nearby grass.

The next morning, the eagle sat perched on his high cliff lookout as usual, enjoying the beauty of the mountains, forest and stream below. In about an hour, he lifted off his perch and began what was becoming a leisurely flight to his favorite fishing spot. The eagle's acceptance that Mother Nature was providing his food without any effort on his part was beginning to develop in him a dull and sluggish nature. He was losing his normal character to be alert.

As the eagle drew near to the rock, he was suddenly puzzled and annoyed. There was an odd structure erected above the rock. He checked his flight and began to soar in circles. He flew fairly high, around and around, trying to make out the strange object. He could see the fish were there as usual. After 20 to 30 minutes of flight, there wasn't any evidence of danger in the bushes near the rock, so he descended to a nearby tree top where he landed. There he spent over an hour in complete silence, observing. His keen eyes kept watch for any strange movement and he listened for any unusual sound. There was nothing!

Far off, however, a good 200 yards away, hidden in the thick bushes, was the motionless trapper, patiently watching every move the eagle made.

After sitting in the treetop for over an hour, the eagle could sense no danger, so he believed it was safe to investigate. He flew down to the shore, landing away from the net. He found a fish in the grass, ate it, grabbed another in his claws, and flew back to his nest. He had not determined that the strange object over the rock was harmless, but it appeared so.

While soaring through the sky that afternoon the eagle couldn't erase from his mind that new object over the rock. He had to know if it was going to interfere with the beautiful way his food had been provided the last couple of weeks. He flew back to the rock and after circling several times, landed on the handle of the net. Nothing happened! The structure appeared to be harmless.

There were still a couple of fish near the rock under the net. He hopped down to test this strange structure. He reached out with his beak and claw clutching one of the fish, then quickly hopped back. The object didn't move.

The next few days the eagle proceeded with caution. With each visit he surveyed the area closely, making sure there was nothing else new. He would move quickly, devouring one fish and carrying a second off to his nest, all the time staying away from the rock.

As the days passed, he regained his confidence that all was well. He was overjoyed that his food was still miraculously being provided. Once again he began to get a fish and perch on the rock, which was directly under the net, to eat his banquet.

The trapper was now ready. Before dawn the next morning, he made some important changes in the arrangement of the net. He tied a strong cord to the rim of the hoop. He ran the cord down to the ground in front of the rock, under a small root, and then ran the cord into the nearby thick bushes. To test the cord, he pulled on it, bending the rim of the net down until it covered the rock.

The trapper satisfied himself all was ready. He baited the trap with the usual fish. Then he moved into the nearby thicket where he had run the cord to wait in silent anticipation.

Right on time, the eagle came the next morning. The trapper watched. The eagle, now full of confidence, had no hesitation. Though wise, he had been deceived into accepting this strange structure and free fish every day as a part of the established order.

He landed on the sand near the rock, grabbed a large fish and perched on the stone under the net to enjoy his meal.

At that very moment, the eagle sensed there was a slight movement in the nearby thicket. His muscles tightened! He was ready to spring into the safety of the air, but before he could move, the four-foot hoop with the net attached came down over him with a vicious swish.

There was an intense battle—the eagle against the net. Beating his wings, tearing at the net with his beak and claws, he fought for his freedom. He strained with every ounce of energy, but soon the eagle became helpless. He was entangled in the mesh of the trap. The mighty and glorious monarch of the sky had fallen to defeat through *deception*.

The story of the eagle demonstrates several principles of *deception*. Most deceptive traps are usually hidden, but there will be visible evidence of their presence. Spiritually, we are warned in the Bible not to believe every spirit, but to try the spirits. *Dear friends, do not believe every spirit, but test the spirits to see whether they are from God …* (I John 4:1). We are to do this by using the Word of God as our guide. That is what Jesus did when Satan tempted him (Matthew 4: 1-11).

The eagle trusted what he saw with his eyes. He ignored his instinct. Adam and Eve were first lured into *deception* by what they saw with their eyes *(the lust of the eyes)* rather than obeying the Word they had from God.

The eagle was drawn to the trap through an appeal to one of his basic needs—food. The deadly temptations of Satan always include an appeal *(the lust of the flesh)* to one of our basic needs. It could be food, clothing, shelter, security, acceptance, position, sex drive and more. These temptations are used as his bait.

The eagle had an inner warning of the hidden dangers, but his desires caused him to go against his wisdom. It is important to spend time in prayer and the Word of God and attend a biblically based

Christian fellowship with solid spiritual leaders and teachers. That is how God provides us with warnings and insights of spiritual danger.

The eagle fell victim to the hidden cost of getting something for nothing. He gained his provision of food every day without labor, but it cost him his natural instinct to be alert.

<u>Satan is a master in tempting us with the pleasure and advantages of sin without revealing the spiritual defeats we will suffer.</u>

The last thing that caused the eagle to fall to *deception* was he became dull and sluggish. He developed a false sense of pride *(pride of life)* in thinking he had all things under control, regardless of the new surroundings. It cost him his freedom. He ended up in bondage.

How easy it is for us to let our guard down and become tolerant of a watered down biblical standard. It is our spiritual pride and false confidence that tells us we can enjoy the pleasures and sins of the world without it hurting us spiritually.

Though contrary to the laws of nature, the eagle accepted new standards because they pleased him. He accepted new standards because they were **self** serving satisfying the flesh. In like manner, the Word of God warns that our spiritual enemy, Satan, will attempt to *deceive* us into accepting other than biblical standards through **self-serving** traps. That was the cause of my downfall. That was the meaning of what the Lord showed me through the vision I had of a large head of a "beast" hovering over America. It was overcoming Christians almost at will through the traps it was able to set through the many temptations coming from our society.

The Bible warns: *Be self-controlled and alert. Your enemy the devil prowls around like a roaring lion looking for someone to devour* (I Peter 5:8).

Deception! It is the tool Satan is using to undermine biblical standards in these last days! This tool of Satan has caused Christians to suffer many spiritual defeats. It is happening throughout America in husband-wife relationships, with children, as well as coping with the pressures and anxieties of life.

To know how our enemy is using the method of *deception* is critical in these last days. This is especially true here in America because we have been the world's center of Christianity. We are being tempted at every turn "to be like God" to determine right and wrong through our own reasoning power.

The eagle became conditioned to his surroundings. He was more interested in satisfying his **selfish** desires. We will examine the areas that make up our **sinful nature** and develops our **selfish** desires in the next chapter. They are being exploited to the fullest extent through our culture as Satan uses the power and influence of the "beast" system to bait his many *deceptive* traps.

Chapter Five

Spiritual Heart Disease

Most everyone is familiar with *physical heart disease*. It quite possibly is the worst plague the world has ever known. It certainly has devastated the United States. It has been reported that over 60 million Americans have one or more forms of heart or blood vessel disease and more than one million suffer a heart attack every year. The estimated cost of cardiovascular disease in America is nearly 100 billion dollars per year when the expense of physician and nursing services, hospital and nursing home care, medications, and lost productivity are tallied.

Physical heart disease has a spiritual counterpart. I call it *spiritual heart disease*. It is the consequence of the heart being overcome by *deception*. *Deception* attacks the inner being of our nature, the mind and our spiritual heart. That is where the toughest battles in spiritual warfare are fought. They are often difficult to detect. Given the power and presence of seducing spirits today, it is important to have a working knowledge of this *spiritual disease*.

Everyone who becomes a Christian, a true believer, becomes a battleground for spiritual warfare. The struggle for control of the believer's thoughts and actions continually takes place. The Holy Spirit of God that we receive at the time of our conversion gives us a new nature (we are spiritually born anew) and empowers us to walk righteously. However, Satan wages war against our new nature by tempting our old **sinful nature**. One of his primary vehicles in this warfare is the deceiving spirits of the world. That is why John writes in I John 2:15,16: *Do not love the world or anything in the world. If anyone loves the world, the love of the Father is not in him. For everything in the world—the cravings of sinful man* (lust of the flesh), *the lust of his eyes and the boasting of what he has and does* (the pride of life)—*comes not from the Father but from the world.* A word study of the word "world" as it is used in these Scriptures is the same as what we call, "society." John is referring to the "things of society."

The Scriptures teach that the temptations of *deception* that we face coming from **the world** or **society** fall into three major categories.

1. *The lust of the flesh.*

2. *The lust of the eyes.*

3. *The pride of life.*

These three areas of man's being make up what Scripture calls our sinful nature. Speaking to Christians, Paul said:

> *As for you, you were dead in your transgressions and sins, in which you used to live when you followed the ways of this world and of the ruler* (Satan) *of the kingdom of the air, the spirit who is now at work in those who are disobedient. All of us also lived among them at one time, gratifying the cravings of our <u>sinful nature</u> and following its desires* (lust) *and thoughts. Like the rest, we were <u>by nature</u> objects of wrath* (Ephesians 2:1-3).

Therefore, just as sin entered the world through one man,
and death through sin, and in this way death came to all men,
because all sinned … (Romans 5:12).

Every person is born with a sinful nature. We didn't ask to have a sinful nature as a part of our inner nature, but the Bible says we did not have a choice. We inherited this nature from the first man, Adam, because of his fall. That is why young children are *naturally* going to lie, cheat, cry or fight as they look after and seek for their **self-interest**. Parents do not purposely teach them to be this way. Everyone is spiritually born on the wrong side of the tracks, so to speak.

Satan is aware that mankind is weak in these three areas that make up our sinful nature; *the lust of the flesh, the lust of the eyes and the pride of life.* Therefore, when attacking the heart through *deception*, he will tempt us in one or all of these three areas.

We see this when Satan tempted and deceived Eve.

When the woman saw that the fruit of the tree was good for food (lust of the flesh) *and pleasing to the eye* (lust of the eye), *and also desirable for gaining wisdom* (pride of life), *she took some and ate it* (Genesis 3:6).

Then the Lord God said to the woman, "What is this you have done?" The woman said, "The serpent (Satan) *deceived me, and I ate"* (Genesis 3:13).

In his temptation of Jesus, Satan tempted Him in the same three areas, trying to cause Him to disobey. This is found in Luke 4:1-13 and Matthew 4:1-11. We examined some of these verses in the previous chapter.

When we yield to the cravings of our sinful nature, its lust and desires, we will seek for **self** interest, **self** satisfaction and **self** glorification.

> *So I say, live by the Spirit* (power of the Holy Spirit within), *and you will not gratify the desires* (lust) *of the <u>sinful nature</u>* (lust of the flesh, lust of the eyes and pride of life). *For the <u>sinful nature</u> desires what is contrary to the Spirit, and the Spirit what is contrary to the <u>sinful nature</u>. They are in conflict with each other, so that you do not do what you want. But if you are led by the Spirit, you are not under law* (Galatians 5:16-18).

The law this verse is referring to is the law of our sinful nature that enjoys sin. It is called the law of sin in Scripture. We are born with an inner nature that causes us to do things we know we shouldn't, and keeps us from doing things we know we should.

After becoming a Christian Paul discovered this law of sin in his inner being. He says: *So I find this law at work: When I want to do good, evil is right there with me. For in my inner being I delight in God's law; but I see another law at work in the members of my body, waging war against the law of my mind and making me a prisoner of the <u>law of sin</u> at work within my members. ... So then, I myself, in my mind am a slave to God's law, but <u>in the sinful nature</u> a slave to the <u>law of sin</u>* (Romans 7:21-25).

Satan knows we have a nature within us that is a slave to the law of sin. He also knows that when we became a Christian, we were given the power of the Holy Spirit to live within. It is a power that is greater than the power of this universal law of sin that is a part of our sinful nature. Romans chapter eight tells us it is only as we are led by the Holy Spirit that we have the power to overcome this natural self-serving law of sin in our being,

Satan's objective then in spiritual warfare is to keep you and me from walking in the power of the Holy Spirit. He knows it is the power of God within that will give us victory over this law of sin in our sinful nature. When Satan is successful and we yield to our sinful nature, Christians will do many things they shouldn't do. They will act no different than the average person in the world and sometimes worse. It also causes us to be very apathetic and *not* do those things we know we should.

Satan accomplishes his objective by tempting the desires of our sinful nature—*the lust of the flesh, the lust of the eyes, and the pride of life*—through the world (society) system in which we live. Observe how often you can identify all three of these desires of our sinful nature being tempted through TV, movie productions, books and magazines, advertisements and many other elements of society. That is the nature of the *deceptive* spiritual warfare we are involved in every day. It is all around us. In our society, primarily because of the advancement of the electronic media, the power of these temptations is greater than any other time in history. We are constantly confronted by the power of the "beast" system.

Understanding Our Sinful Nature

To comprehend the strategy behind Satan's *deceptive* warfare, it will help if we take a closer look at the weaknesses of our sinful nature.

The three areas that make up our sinful nature, *the lust of the flesh, the lust of the eyes and the pride of life* includes things that are pleasing to our **self-life** regardless of the act. It is the primary desire to satisfy "good 'ol me!"

The lust of the flesh and the eyes might include things such as sexual drive, food, material things and pleasures. There is nothing wrong with any of these things within themselves. It is when our lust or desire for these things is so powerful it causes us to disobey the standards of God's Word that they become wrong. For example, if our desire for material things or pleasures cause us to use white lies (manipulation), deceitful tactics, not paying bills when due, being dishonest, greedy, not tithing properly, viewing or partaking in pleasurable things that are sinful, and so on. We are going to be tempted by the standards of society to use these practices as our rule of conduct for the purpose of obtaining materialistic benefits or gratifying our fleshly nature. But, as Jesus did when He was tempted, we too must learn to stand against temptation with the Word of God.

Please note that I am not trying to discount any of God's blessings in one's life or any of the provisions He may supply. However, we need to be aware that Satan uses the world system to tempt our natural desires. That is a strong biblical teaching.

One way to know whether a material item is a blessing from God or one of Satan's traps—something of the world—is to examine its effects. Will the item cause me to sin in any way by the way I have to obtain it, or could it cause me to neglect God's will for my life after I obtain it?

Remember that the fish offered to the eagle was his normal diet. However, the fall came later, due to his becoming dull and lazy. Examine again the temptations of Jesus in (Matthew 4:1-11). They appear to be harmless, not causing Jesus to break any of God's Word. But being alert He knew they were not within the will of God and the after effects would bring sinful results because they appealed only to His self-serving interest.

Satan's objective is to tempt us with material things that will cause us to sin. Sin quenches the power of the Holy Spirit in our lives. And when we are not walking in God's power the law of our sin nature, our own selfish desires, will control our actions. I think you can identify with what I am saying because it is our sinful nature that causes us to become irritated, angry, boastful, conceited, haughty, proud, disrespectful to others, selfish, self-centered, wanting our own way, speaking unkind words about others, having immoral thoughts and much more. The list is virtually inexhaustible.

In the same way the trapper caught the eagle, Satan uses material things to lure us into one of his traps. When caught, that quenches the power of the Holy Spirit in controlling our lives. Our world system is one of the most powerful ever to exist in offering this type of *deceitful* temptation.

Another way Satan uses the world system to tempt our sinful nature is to create a desire in us for *excessive pleasure.*

He will tempt us to <u>over commit</u> our time to do pleasurable things, or to be entertained by pleasurable things that are sinful. The many resources at Satan's disposal in America today create an unbelievable temptation for most of us in this area. I am not against good and wholesome things like enjoying God's creation and its beauty, the company of friends, playing wholesome games and so forth. But the enemy is attacking us fiercely in the area of the *lust of the flesh and eyes* to enjoy the pleasures developed and produced by our society system.

One of the strongest temptations is the way Satan's demons are capitalizing on man's sinful and natural tendency to immorality through the eyes. They are using every available means. Immodest dress, impure magazines, pornographic books and pictures, and many of the TV and movie productions are evidence of it. A discerning person who glances at the newsstands, reads the advertisements on the theater page of the newspaper or watches the programs and commercials presented on television, knows full well that the *lust of the eyes and the flesh* is being exploited by the power of the devil. Anyone can walk into a store and see the covers of pornographic or suggestive magazines openly being displayed. Or what about the immoral TV and movie productions that are made available to anyone who will pay the price or give them the time. Why do you think there are so many and that they have been made to be so attractive and entertaining? Look at their message. Most of them are made to attract and stir up that which makes up our sinful nature.

Their effect has been devastating to our society as sex, crime, terrorism and violence have become a steady diet for the majority, exploding through most every medium of entertainment.

Look at sex! A result is that Christians have developed an apathetic attitude toward God's standards of sex and have become receptive to society's standards. For example: Christian couples live together before marriage; have sex while dating; adultery is practiced; immodest dress is hardly ever mentioned; there are thousands of illegitimate children in Christian families; and disregard for marriage vows has reached epidemic levels. In the world, venereal and other social diseases have reached epidemic proportions occurring more often than any other infectious disease except the common cold; we have killed over 40 million lives through abortion; homosexuality is openly discussed and taught as an acceptable lifestyle. And there are many other sinful things to countless to name that have become a part of our everyday lifestyle.

Though it is seldom talked about, one of the greatest effects on Christian men is the overwhelming number who have become addicted to pornography. It has become a national plague. I know women do not understand this, but as they examine the Scriptures they can see that sex has always been an area of constant spiritual warfare for men. With the electronic media available today and the standards of society that allows so much exposure to things of a sexual nature, the power of this temptation has overtaken many Christian men.

My brother, Bob Fraley, was recently on a long trip riding on an airplane when suddenly the young man sitting next to him grabbed a pen and note pad and began to write rapidly. He wrote very quickly without stopping until he had finished. At the time my brother could not help but notice how quickly the young man was writing. He thought to himself: *"This young man is certainly inspired in what he is writing."* Because of this he was definitely interested in what was being written. After the young man had finished he handed to my brother what he had written. My brother had no idea of the young man's struggles nor did the young man have any idea my brother was helping me write this book. I am going to share what this young committed Christian man wrote. It will help open your eyes to the power of this temptation of pornography. He wrote:

My whole life I have been raised up in the circle and teachings of Jesus. I can never remember the day that I have not had the thought of Jesus in my mind.

My parents are Christians. My brothers, sisters, aunts, uncles, grand-parents and schoolteachers have all been Christians. Christianity has always surrounded me. So it is no surprise that I am a dedicated Christian.

I originally gave my life to Christ when I was little, but over the years I have rededicated my life to Him. I have especially done this when things in my life were taking a downfall.

I have always tried to live my life in a way that would be pleasing to my parents and also to Christ. But I really feel that over the last five to six years my spiritual life has taken a downfall.

I have been so blessed my whole life, not only materially, but also with my family. I have always felt the comfort and the ability of coming before my family with any problems or questions. God has allowed me to be honest in my struggles and not allow my pride to get in the way of telling people my problems.

Over the last few years the Lord has <u>not</u> really been the main focus of my life, and it is now coming to a point where I can feel my heart is becoming hard. Being raised in a Christian home I have been extremely sheltered my whole life. I never really went through the struggles with worldliness while I was young. It took longer for me to realize all of the different stuff that the world had to offer. I really started to realize all the different things that the world had to offer in college.

Basically my problems started when my roommate and myself rented a movie. In this movie it had a brief scene of nudity which basically was my first time seeing that in a movie. I have to admit I liked it but didn't really think too much of it. After that movie my friend and I would rent other movies that would also have scenes of nudity and with each one I saw I liked it more and more at the time, but yet felt worse and worse every time I saw it.

At first I was more curious than anything else, but after a while it became more than curiosity. It became something I liked because it turned me on and fed my flesh. At this time in my life I didn't curse, I didn't drink, I didn't smoke, and I read my Bible every night. By the time I left college I had done all of these things and I wasn't reading my Bible.

Things started to get worse with my addiction to pornography. I started to rent "R" rated movies on my own, and watched them by myself, and would return them feeling really guilty. I would never watch really bad ones with my friends because I didn't want them to know I was like them, because they didn't seem to have a problem with it. But then I would take the movies that they rented and watch them by myself and then give them back to them. Like it was better that I wasn't watching it with them. I had a real problem starting up with these movies because I had been trained differently and I didn't realize the consequences that it would have on my life.

Things just got worse as time went on. The problem didn't go away. I still had the fleshly desire and the same results after I would watch a "R" rated movie. And then sooner or later I really didn't feel too bad after I did it. Pleasing my self with these movies became a regular routine, and during these times I was seeing my spiritual life go down the drain. I wasn't allowing God to work in my life at all. Satan had definitely found a way to get into my life, and I had allowed it to happen.

One problem that I really see with pornography is that nobody wants to talk about it. One thing that happens if somebody is an alcoholic or on drugs is it usually becomes obvious. When people find out that somebody is struggling with either of these problems they can immediately get help. But pornography is a disease that Satan is using on today's Christian men and it is destroying them and I know this from experience. Satan is quietly *finding a way to creep into Christian homes without anybody knowing about it, especially with the availability of the Internet that we have today.*

One deception that Satan hit me with is that all of my problems with pornography would be over with once I got married which did not happen. Even though I got married my problems and struggles still carried on. And it definitely caused other problems because I have been able to tell my wife about my struggles, and she is praying for me and trying to understand how this happens. She can't understand that it has nothing to do with her and how she is not pleasing me. The only thing that causes this is Satan and his desire for me to follow my flesh.

Once I got married my wife and I got the Internet to help with her job of teaching school, and that put a whole new perspective on my struggles. The easiness and quickness of pornography was unreal. Once again it started out as a curiosity and then led into more that that. It eventually turned into something I enjoyed, but would still feel guilty after I was done watching it. I would try and try to quit and would accomplish that desire for a few weeks, but after that Satan would win and I would give in and look at more things. I was losing the spiritual battle that Christ wanted me to win.

Then one Sunday I went to church and heard a man speak on his struggles and one of them was pornography. After he was done speaking he asked for an altar call, in which I went forward bawling like a baby. Then a great thing happened in my life. I allowed Christ to work in my life again and I was winning the battle. The speaker, Carl, and I would meet once a week to talk about things and I was starting to grow again and was starting to get over the desire to look at things that I shouldn't. Things were finally starting to go better for me with my struggle. Then I graduated from the Christian college I attended and had to leave. My relationship with Carl faded and I started to waiver again. After moving from where I attended college I again started to look at pornography here and there and started to go back into the groove of what I was doing before.

I have tried so many times in my life to stop looking at this stuff, but it just doesn't happen. I am at a point right now in my life that I am losing the battle again, and I am failing the spiritual battle that my whole life has been brought up to win. My wife has been by my side through this, but it hasn't really helped her or me. I am still losing. I look at pornography at different times whether at work on the Internet or at home on TV or some movies. I am dying inside and I don't know what I can do about it. I feel that I try to allow God to help me but I must <u>not</u> be doing it enough because I just can't seem to win.

There was a time where I felt that Christ was calling me to minister to younger adults about this struggle and the different things that it entails. But I have let that slip through the cracks. Now I am at a point in my life where I don't know where to turn. I want to turn to Christ but Satan tells me it isn't working and that no matter how hard I try I still fail. I just can't stay away from looking at these things I know I shouldn't, and when I decide to do it Satan allows for something to come my way to make it real easy for me to see.

I feel like I need to stop but I just feel like I can't. I want to tell others to stay away from this struggle, but how can I tell them when I can't do it myself.

The Lord has to have some master plan for my life and me because I love Him too much to allow pornography to ruin my relationship with Him. I try so hard to live a good life, and this is the biggest struggle that I have. I am not sure where to go from here, but I know the Lord wants me to go somewhere away from pornography. I just don't know how that is *going to happen because the Lord knows that I have tried so hard to get away from this addiction and it just hasn't happened. Pornography is ruining my life and I feel like there is nothing I can do about it.*

Bill McCartney, President and Founder of Promise Keepers, recently told my brother that pornography was one of the worse temptations Christian men in America have to deal with. Privately, most men, especially young men, in our society confess it is a difficult temptation for them to handle, yet it is hardly being addressed. You don't hear about it from the pulpit or in Bible studies.

In *my testimony* I reviewed that I had fallen from a very strong temptation. Although the cause of my defeat was different, it was not pornography, the principle of being restored is the same. It only came with spending a tremendous amount of time in the Word of God and prayer. It required filling my mind and heart with the things of God rather than with the things of this world. That was the only way I found the power of the Holy Spirit, which is necessary to overcome the temptations coming from the world system. The young man's comment about being honest, confessing his problem and keeping it surfaced, is also an important part of this process of gaining victory.

King David's guidance in dealing with some of these issues we are confronted with today states: *I will sing of your love and justice; to you, O Lord, I will sing praise. I will be careful to lead a blameless life— when will you come to me? I will walk in my house with blameless heart. I will set before my eyes no vile thing. The deeds of faithless men I hate; they will not cling to me. Men of perverse heart shall be far from me; I will have nothing to do with evil* (Psalm 101:1-4).

We are under tremendous pressures to yield to excessive pleasure and materialism in these last days. We are bombarded daily to accept the standards of the world as never before over God's standards. The effect is that families are suffering from the many struggles it has caused, and many are falling apart. Emotional stress and depression are at record levels. Americans suffering from emotional or mental problems are at an all time high.

The **third** part that makes up our sinful nature is *the pride of life*. Society tempts the natural sinful characteristic of *the lust of the flesh, the lust of the eyes and the pride of life*.

The *pride of life* is wanting to be somebody. It is expressed through our desire to be noticed, be seen, be exalted, be important, be popular, be right, and be esteemed. Our culture goes to extreme measures to influence us to exert maximum effort for money, applause, recognition, and position. The struggle for power, prestige and honor is at the heart of almost every human endeavor including many of the good things that are done. The Bible says the nature of Jesus had no personal ambition of His own. He said: *I tell you the truth, the Son can do nothing by himself; he can do only what he sees his Father doing, because whatever the Father does the Son also does* (John 5:19). Also: *By myself I can do nothing; I judge only as I hear, and my judgment is just, for I seek not to please myself but him who sent me* (John 5:30).

The characteristic of pride in the American people has definitely become a problem and made a heavy contribution to the moral conditions we now find in our country. Pride stands in the way of true love, the giving of oneself, which is the nature and character of God (see I Corinthians 13:4.)

Above everything else, it is our *pride* that hinders God's grace from flowing in our lives. It is a part of the "old man," the "old na-

103

ture" that needs to be broken. A heart God revives is a humble and broken heart. *The sacrifices of God are a broken spirit; a broken and contrite heart, O God, you will not despise* (Psalm 51:17). God says: ... *I hate pride and arrogance* ... (Proverbs 8:13). *Pride only breeds quarrels* ... (Proverbs 13:10). *The Lord detests all the proud of heart...* (Proverbs 16:5). *Before his downfall a man's heart is proud* ... (Proverbs 18:12). *Live in harmony with one another. Do not be proud, but be willing to associate with people of low position. Do not be conceited* (Romans 12:16). *... God opposes the proud but gives grace to the humble* (James 4:6). We are to become completely dependent on God. Human nature does not like to be dependent on something or someone else. Pride has become one of our greatest spiritual problems in the American church.

Ulitmate Development

The Bible teaches the social structure of this world is controlled by a prevailing principle of life that is foreign to God and leads people away from Him. This principle penetrates education, literature, science, business, religion, economics, politics, government, medicine, entertainment, and any other segment that makes up society.

Satan uses the material world, the people of the world, and the value systems of the world. Our society has been exalted far above all other societies giving it great power in all areas of worldly influence to tempt and try to *deceive* Christians so that we will become independent and step outside of God's Word.

No longer is it necessary for you and me to go into the world in order to make contact with it. The influences of our society come and search us out. Its forces are so strong that it captivates people daily. Never before has the Christian family felt the power and pull of a worldly society to conform to its ways. Our apathy toward the many areas of lawlessness in our society reveals we are willing to let Satan and the world do practically anything as long as it doesn't affect our bank accounts.

Wherever you go, even among Christians, the things of the world are usually the topic of conversation. Most conversations are centered on food, clothing, housing, pleasure, buying, the deals we've made, the items we've purchased, or the pleasures in which we have been involved. The powerful influence of our society has caused Christians to place a greater emphasis on supplying the physical needs and wants of our families than in supplying their spiritual needs.

We all have been in the bondage of sin and readily agree that sinful things are from Satan, <u>but we do not equally believe that many things of the world are of Satan</u>. Yet the Scriptures clearly affirm that: *... the whole world* (societies) *is under the control of the evil one* (I John 5:19). Many are still of two minds about this.

Satan knows that to influence and deceive Christians through activities that are clearly sinful will often be vain and futile. The Bible does not teach this is his normal method. He is much wiser than that. He knows the majority of Christians will usually sense these dangers and flee. Instead, he has developed an enticing worldly society, the mesh of which is so skillfully woven so as to entrap the most innocent of people.

We live in the world and are to convert the things out of the world, but only to bring glory to God. The cross of Christ has shattered all of our hope in the things that this world has to offer. Satan uses every trick possible to deceive and destroy this kind of thinking.

Paul said: *May I never boast except in the cross of our Lord Jesus*

Christ, through which the world has been crucified to me, and I to the world (Galatians 6:14).

The key to our victory is always our faith relationship with the victorious Son. *I have told you these things, so that in me you may have peace. In this world you will have trouble. But take heart! I have overcome the world* (John 16:33). ... *in this world we are like him* (I John 4:17b). Jesus is the only one who ever overcame the pressures and influences of the world. The depth of our victory is completely dependent upon Christ Jesus and the faith we have in Him living His life in and through us. There is no room for any victory through **self**.

Chapter Six

Spirit Of Lawlessness

The purpose of this chapter is not for me to convince you that America is a lawless society. That is revealed every day by listening to the news or reading the newspaper. The American society is a society where you don't know from one day to the next what unspeakable crime is going to be reported. And all the crimes committed are not by hardened thugs. Even children are going on killing sprees gunning down other children and teachers at school. I guess we shouldn't be surprised knowing that many children have watched thousands of murders on television and have been taught there are no moral absolutes, so they see little harm in killing their classmates.

The purpose of this chapter is to look at God's warning in Scripture that reveals the root cause of the "spirit of lawlessness" that we are experiencing in our country.

Statistics confirm that the American people have become the world's most immoral people even though we live in the world's greatest geographical center of Christian teaching. That is hard to understand. This fact says more than anything else that Christians are not living by the moral standards taught in the Bible. The freedom to openly commit sin in America is a reflection on the body of Christ.

Our spiritual weakness and lack of spiritual commitment for righteousness is revealed in that *many Americans no longer have a fear of sinning.* Christians have become so much a part of the world we don't cause conviction in the people anymore.

Every single Christian is being called to fight in the army of God in the spiritual warfare now taking place in our country. There is no way you can avoid it! The Lord is depending on you, and me, to show the world whose God has the power—theirs or ours! The only way we are going to keep our society from becoming more and more evil, and sinking deeper and deeper into sin is to take a stand.

God has given Christians in America a rich Christian heritage along with the freedom to live out our faith. It is obvious Satan is out to destroy every good thing with which God has blessed us.

The Lord gave the Apostle Paul a prophetic word about the lawless spirit that would sweep across the central area of Christianity in the end-times. It reveals the root cause and nature of the "spirit of lawlessness" that Satan has developed in our country. In II Thessalonians 2:1-4 Paul writes:

> *Concerning the coming of our Lord Jesus Christ and our being gathered to him, we ask you, brothers, not to become easily unsettled or alarmed by some prophecy, report or letter supposed to have come from us, saying that the day of the Lord has already come. Don't let anyone deceive you in any way, for that day will not come* (the return of Jesus) *until the rebellion occurs and the man of lawlessness is revealed, the man doomed to destruction. He opposes and exalts himself over everything that is called God*

or is worshiped, and even sets himself up in God's temple, pro-claiming himself to be God.

Paul's opening statement in these verses: *Concerning the coming of our Lord Jesus Christ and our being gathered to him,* establishes the fact that he is talking about the last days, the second coming of Jesus—the time in which we are now living.

Paul then reveals two profound things that must happen before Jesus will return. He says **first** *the rebellion* must occur and **second** *the man of lawlessness* must be revealed.

The Greek word used in this verse for rebellion is apostasia. It means to defect or fall away. To fall into apostasy is to abandon or renounce a belief in following the standards of biblical Christianity. We may wrap ourselves up in the act of Christian service, but our lifestyle reveals that we are no longer committed to the standards of Christ. This is the type of falling away Paul is talking about. That is what happened to me!

In using the word apostasy (falling away), Paul is <u>not</u> implying that dedicated Christians won't make their share of mistakes. That is not his point! He knows that is going to happen. By using the word apostasy he is warning that in the last days many who go by the name of Christian will fall away from being committed to obey true biblical standards. That was my experience!

Paul continues his prophetic warning about our day in the third verse. He calls those who fall away from following the standards of God a *man of lawlessness.* In modern English a more suitable phrase might be to call such a person a **lawless man.** Paul uses the phrase *man of lawlessness* because from a biblical viewpoint anyone who does not respect the laws of God is a person with a **lawless spirit.**

The "spirit of lawlessness" Paul is talking about must develop in a society of strong Christian teaching. Otherwise, how can there be a **falling away** from Christian standards, as he points out, if they were not first the prominent standards being followed by that society? How can you fall from something if you were not there first?

It is a well-known fact that America has been the center of Christian activity in these last days. Our country was established on many of the Christian principles found in the Bible. Our constitution was based on Christian standards. In the past we were referred to as a Christian nation. "In God we trust," is printed on our money. The majority of American people used Christian standards to live by until recent years.

But in this last generation that all began to change. Our society started to move away from following many of the Christian standards taught in the Bible. Rebellion against many of God's laws took hold. The "spirit of lawlessness" in man began to take over and change the laws that govern our land. This has developed in the people a **lawless spirit** towards the standards of God. It is why so many people in America have the attitude that they have the right to decide right from wrong for themselves. Our nation has moved from honoring God's standards on how we should live to where the majority of people now rely on their own personal taste to decide proper living standards. That is literally taking the place of God. It is a "spirit of lawlessness."

America is the only society in the world in these last days that meets the full description of Paul's prophetic warning. The majority of the people who once followed God's standards have now fallen from following many of these standards. Therefore, we can conclude his warning must apply to the United States as much or more so than to any other country.

In verse 4 Paul tells us how Satan has developed the spirit of rebellion or lawlessness against God's standards in the minds of the people. It reads: *He* (which refers to the man with a lawless spirit) *opposes and exalts himself* (his own person) *over everything that is called God or is worshiped, and even sets himself up in God's temple, proclaiming himself to be God.*

The pronoun *himself* occurs three times in this verse. That is the key! It defines the method of seduction the "beast" society is using to bring about the "spirit of lawlessness." It is the cause of the rebellion or falling away from Christian standards that Paul mentions in verse 3. It is the spiritual reason why a "spirit of lawlessness" has swept over our nation like a flood in the last generation. It has been the process of man setting *himself* up—good ole' me, myself, and I—to decide right from wrong and serve myself as though I was a god.

The Bible says that Satan had this same attitude and it is why God cast him out of Heaven. Speaking of Satan, God's Word states: *You said in your heart, "I will ascend to heaven; I will raise my throne above the stars of God; I will sit enthroned on the mount of assembly, on the utmost heights of the sacred mountain. I will ascend above the tops of the clouds; I will make myself like the Most High"* (Isaiah 14:13,14). "I," "I," "I," I will do this, I will do that. I will be my own god. I will decide right from wrong! That is rebellion! That is lawlessness!

It is how verse 4 describes the falling away, and the *man of lawlessness* it speaks of in verse 3. And he is not talking about just one man. He is talking about the general frame of mind that develops in the people, including many Christians, towards biblical Christian standards.

This prophetic warning from Paul is powerful! It answers a major question that has appeared in this last generation and puzzled most Christians. The question is: How could America, with such a strong Christian foundation, and where so much Christian teaching has taken place, be experiencing such a rapid increase in the spirit of lawlessness, permissiveness, rebellion and selfishness? A condition that has continued to get worse over the last 30 to 40 years and is now completely out of control. And nothing—new programs, education, or anything else—seems to have any effect in changing what is happening.

Where have we gone wrong? Paul answers that question in verse 4. The falling away or rebellion in our society has occurred because we are guilty of taking the place of God's Word by setting ourselves up to make our own moral decisions. That is what Paul prophesied would happen. We are guilty of doing the same thing Satan did in saying: *I will make myself like the Most High.*

To quote verse 4 again: *He* (which refers to the lawless man in verse 3) *opposes and exalts himself* (his own being) *over everything that is called God* (God's standards) *or is worshiped, and even sets himself up in God's temple, proclaiming himself to be God* (decides right from wrong). Where does Paul say man sets himself up? In the *temple* of God! Where is the *temple* of God in Christianity? Scripture says it is man's body.

There are those who teach Paul's use of the word *temple* in verse 4 is speaking about the *temple* in Jerusalem. To be sure he is talking about the human body, and not the *temple* in Jerusalem, a word study was done on the word, *temple*. It was found he is talking about the human body.

There are two Greek words in Scripture that are translated *temple*. One is **hieron** and usually refers to the *temple* in Jerusalem. The other is **naos** and sometimes refers to the heart of the *temple* in Jerusalem, but when used in Christianity the Greek word **naos** always refers to the body of man being the *temple* of God.

For example, all three of the following verses from Corinthians state that the body of man is the *temple* of God. In each verse the Greek word **naos** is used for *temple*.

> *Don't you know that you yourselves are God's temple* (the Greek word naos is used for temple) *and that God's Spirit lives in you?* (I Corinthians 3:16).

> *Do you not know that your body is a temple* (naos is used) *of the Holy Spirit, who is in you, whom you have received from God?* (I Corinthians 6:19).

> *What agreement is there between the temple of God and idols? For we are the temple* (naos is used) *of the living God* (II Corinthians 6:16).

The same was found to be true when Jesus said: ..."*Destroy this temple* (the Greek word used is naos), *and I will raise it again in three days.*" *The Jews replied, "It has taken forty-six years to build this temple, and you are going to raise it in three days?" But the temple he had spoken of was his body* (John 2:19-21). When the human body is referred to as the *temple* of God throughout the New Testament, you will find the Greek word **naos** is used for *temple*.

113

In II Thessalonians 2:1-4, Scripture is warning people that live in the last days that a rebellion or falling away will take place. The cause of the falling away is man will set *himself* up in the *temple* of God and serve himself as though he is a god. In verse 4 Paul used the Greek word **naos,** not **hieron,** for *temple.* He is talking about the human body not the *temple* in Jerusalem. That makes perfect sense because Paul is writing to Christians and in Christianity mankind is the *temple.*

In other countries many people serve false gods. But they do not serve themselves as though they were their own god. They make great personal sacrifices to these false gods.

The power of the "beast" system in our society has developed tremendous resources to produce and make available many goods and services for the people to serve themselves. Our electronic media—TV, the Internet, movies, and the press—has tremendous power to influence us to accept worldly standards and decide right from wrong for ourselves. These elements that exist today are something the Christian community has never had to contend with before this last generation. They have created a powerful temptation for everyone to serve themselves as a god more than any time I can think of in the history of mankind.

Though the majority of Christians in our country once respected and tried to live by the laws of God, today many have rebelled by developing a **lawless spirit** towards many of God's laws so they can do the things they want. The moral standards taught in the Bible that once were normal have been discarded. We have placed our own desires above our regard for God's laws so we can cater to our own self-interest. Right from wrong has become a matter of personal taste. We have set ourselves up in the *temple* of God—the human body—taking the place of God by the way we make our own moral decisions so we can serve ourselves.

II Thessalonians 2:4 is a perfect description of the religion of humanism and the new age movement. It has swept through our country in recent years and has become the main philosophy taught in our schools. It is the primary standard by which the majority of people now live.

Using the powerful influence of the "beast" society to tempt us to serve ourselves like a god, above the true God, is the vehicle Satan has used to seduce and deceive the American Christian. It fits Paul's description of *the man of lawlessness* in verse 4.

In this prophetic warning from Paul, it tells Christians that the most important thing you and I need to be concerned about in the spiritual warfare we face today is not the open and blatant sins we see taking place. We are being seduced and deceived by the power of our society to serve ourselves above what is normal. That is the deceptive trick Satan is using. He is tempting us by appealing to a basic need or attracting us to something that appears good and legitimate. He won't usually try to engage us in some gross sin that we can easily detect. However, be assured he is going to set his traps for the Christian in his endeavor to get us to fall away. You can count on that! *Deception*, working through all of the attractions of the "beast" society has been his method in America. It is very similar to those methods used by the trapper to deceive and catch the eagle.

Jesus adds considerable insight to these deceptive methods of Satan. He warns us about the last days and the type of spiritual warfare we are talking about. He compares our times to the days of Noah and to Lot's day. He said:

> *Just as it was in the days of Noah, so also will it be in the days of the Son of Man. People were eating, drinking, marrying and being given in marriage up to the day Noah entered the ark. Then the flood came and destroyed them all. It was the same in the days of Lot. People were eating and drinking, buying and selling, planting and building. But the day Lot left Sodom, fire and sulfur rained down from heaven and destroyed them all. It will be just like this on the day the Son of Man is revealed* (Luke 17:26-30).

Do you notice something missing in this passage of Scripture? Jesus doesn't mention the many evil and gross sins that were taking place in Noah's day or Lot's day? Nor does He say anything about the many gross sins taking place in our day. In fact, not one of the things He warns us about in this prophetic passage of Scripture is a sin within themselves. They are the everyday normal things people do in living this life: drinking, eating, marrying, buying, selling, planting and building.

Take marriage for example! The basic institution of marriage is certainly not wrong. It is specifically created and highly honored by the Lord. It was at a wedding that Jesus performed His first miracle. But the attitude that many have developed today about the sanctity of marriage is wrong. It is our attitude toward the way that we are now handling the everyday affairs of life that Jesus is talking about.

The Old Testament Scriptures state that in the days of Noah and Lot there was violence such as the world had never seen, gross immorality, homosexuality, and many other gross sins. But Jesus doesn't mention any of those things.

Why does Jesus focus only on the legitimate things people were doing in Noah's day? Why didn't He mention our present day immorality, crime, violence, the drug epidemic, over-crowded jails, homosexuality, or abortion? It is because He had a greater concern. Jesus is saying that our day has become the same as it was in the days of Noah in that we have become so wrapped up and engrossed in those things that pertain to the every day affairs of life <u>we are guilty of neglecting the standards of God to serve ourselves</u>. That can be a very *deceptive* form of lawlessness.

Jesus is warning that the commitment of the hearts of the people in the time of Noah to their everyday affairs of life caused their hearts to grow so cold they began to fall away from following the standards of God. He is saying the same will be true in our day.

Christians have become too occupied with the problems of this life. We even develop anxiety over such ordinary matters as food and dress. People in our society are caught up in a whirlwind of buying that is unprecedented. Our present state of affairs is not natural to man, as history bears out.

There is a super, hidden satanic power, which seems to captivate people every day, causing them to lose sight of their priorities concerning material goods. It can be noticed everywhere! The problem is not how to refrain from the buying, selling and eating, but how to avoid this satanic power in our society which has changed the course of man's response and commitment. Our attachment to the things of the world is abnormal Christian behavior. We are meeting the work of demons. The present state of buying cannot be accounted for in any other way. Christians need to wake up to this point because it can open the door for *deception* to ensnare us into Satan's worldly traps.

Jesus knew all about the terrible sins that took place in Noah's day, as well as the crime, violence, sexual permissiveness, abortion, child abuse and other sins that would be going on in our world today. Yet when comparing our day to those days of Noah and Lot, Jesus does not make one comment about this fact.

The purpose of Jesus comparing the everyday normal affairs of life in the time of Noah to our day takes us to the very core of the spiritual warfare we see taking place in America. It is why the moral values of our society have deteriorated so quickly. It pinpoints the method of seduction the enemy is using to cause the "spirit of lawlessness" to serve me, myself, and I, like a god, that Paul prophesied about in II Thessalonians 2:1-4.

By putting the comments of Jesus and Paul together, we learn that we may be doing good and legitimate things. But if we become overcommitted to the everyday affairs of life and use them to serve ourselves over and above our service to God, then we will lose our spiritual discernment. We will become like the eagle. These things mentioned by Jesus become bait for the enemy to cause us to grow cold towards the standards of God.

When God warns His people, it usually deals with an area that is not obvious to human wisdom. It covers a subject that requires the Lord's insight. His warnings are directed towards areas that the enemy is using to *deceive* us. Areas that can take us out from under the Lord's hedge of protection and could possibly hurt or destroy us spiritually—even though His warnings are often something we don't like to hear or want to talk about.

The Lord's main concern in this warning that compares our day to Noah's and Lot's day is for the majority of people—people like you and me. All who go about doing those things that people do in the normal way of living their life—the buying, selling, building, marrying, and so forth. It carries a much deeper and far greater concern than the many gross sins now taking place. Everyone knows about the many gross sins. We don't have to be warned about that!

Jesus could see into the future and He prophesied that our lives would become dominated by the everyday affairs of life. In these days of great prosperity we are so busy with our everyday affairs many cannot see that we are in the middle of a spiritual warfare that has developed a very self-centered, self-serving people.

The focus of the warning from Jesus is with the attitude of the heart that He saw in the majority. That is why He lists the things that have to do with our everyday affairs even though not one of them is a sin within itself. What we are doing is not the sin that is taking us out from under the hedge of God's protection and quenching the power of the Holy Spirit in our lives. It is the commitment of our hearts to the self-serving things of everyday life over and above our commitment to the standards of God.

Jesus is warning us that we will become so occupied with these things that serve ourselves—the buying, selling, building, eating, planting, marrying and giving in marriage, everyday things—that we lose our values in knowing right from wrong concerning these things. As it was in the days of Noah, our commitment to these things has caused us to lose our discernment in interpreting the signs of the times. This has become a deceptive snare in our society because of its overpowering ability to influence our lives. It has created in us a "spirit of lawlessness" towards following many of the standards of God. This condition has become a very serious problem for Christians.

God chose to put these words of warning from Jesus in the Bible. God is faithful. It was important to Him that we know the kind of spiritual warfare the enemy would throw at Christians in these end-times.

Jesus said very little about the times in which we now live. Or if He did it was not recorded in Scripture. That means if something He said about our times did make it on the pages of the Bible, God is telling us it is important that we understand what is being said.

Jesus did many other things as well. If every one of them were written down, I suppose that even the whole world would not have room for the books that would be written (John 21:25). If everything Jesus said and did was recorded, the Bible makes a point about it being so much that it caused John to suppose the whole world would not have room for the books that would be written.

Most of what Jesus said and did <u>was not</u> recorded in the Bible. Therefore, if something Jesus said was recorded in the Bible, then we can be sure it is important to God that you and I take it to heart. That is why these verses from Luke about comparing the days of Noah and Lot to our day are so critical for the body of Christ today.

Of all the things Jesus could have said about the times in which we live, the one that God chose to record and has passed on to warn us about our day are these verses in Luke 17:26-30. That makes this warning extremely significant.

Chapter Seven

Christian Character

Our self-seeking pursuits and careless living have led to a great problem in our society. It is the overall lack of respect for the standards of God. That was a major aspect of spiritual deterioration in Noah's day and what caused the falling away. According to Scripture it is a great concern for God today. **It has changed the character of the American people.**

The moral structure of our society is collapsing, and Christians are doing very little to stand firm and fight against the problem. In this last generation the availability of so many things of the world has created a temptation for Christians, which is unprecedented in the history of mankind. It is beyond one's imagination. Add to that the fact of how easy credit is obtained. This makes it even more difficult for people to avoid falling into Satan's worldly trap of becoming over committed to the everyday affairs of life.

To find the real reason behind the corruption and violence in our nation we need to look at ourselves. Our hearts are no longer in tune with the heart of God. This is what has brought about the bitter harvest of suffering and defeat that we are experiencing in our country today. We have allowed Satan to undermine our families, our public schools, our government, our way of thinking, and our social order. This is well illustrated by a prayer that was recently written by a high school student that loves the Lord. It reads:

Now I sit me down in school, where praying is against the rule.

For this great nation under God, finds mention of Him very odd.

If Scripture now the class recites, it violates the Bill of Rights.

And anytime my head I bow, becomes a federal matter now.

Our hair can be purple or orange or green, that's no offense, it's the freedom scene.

The law is specific, the law is precise, prayers spoken aloud are a serious vice.

For praying in a public hall, might offend someone with no faith at all.

In silence alone we must meditate, God's name is prohibited by the State.

We're allowed to cuss and dress like freaks, and pierce our noses, tongues and checks.

They've outlawed guns; but first the Bible, to quote the Good Book makes me liable.

We can elect a pregnant Senior Queen, and the unwed daddy, our Senior King.

It's "inappropriate" to teach right from wrong, we're taught that such "judgments" do not belong.

We can get our condoms and birth controls, study witchcraft, vampires and totem poles.

But the Ten Commandments are not allowed, no Word of God must reach this crowd.

It's scary here, I must confess, when chaos reigns, the schools a mess.

So Lord, this silent plea I make: Should I be shot, my soul to take.

We have exchanged the commitment of our heart to righteousness for a spirit of tolerance towards the ways of the world. Jesus said: *For where your treasure is, there your heart will be also* (Matthew 6:21). And: *But the things that come out of the mouth come from the heart, and these make a man 'unclean.' For out of the heart come evil thoughts, murder, adultery, sexual immorality, theft, false testimony, slander* (Matthew 15:18,19).

It is what comes out of *the heart* that reveals our character. Satan knows the heart is where we are most vulnerable. He is out to win the battle for control over the hearts of as many Christians in America as possible. *The heart is deceitful above all things ...* (Jeremiah 17:9). This is reflected in our character.

The Apostle Paul wrote to Timothy about the character of Christians in the last days. He said: *But mark this: There will be terrible times in the last days. People will be lovers of themselves, lovers of money, boastful, proud, abusive, disobedient to their parents, ungrateful, unholy (immoral), without love, unforgiving, slanderous, without self-control, brutal, not lovers of the good, treacherous, rash, conceited, lovers of pleasure rather than lovers of God—having a form of godliness but denying its power. Have nothing to do with them* (II Timothy 3:1-5).

Paul lists several characteristics of the heart in these verses. They will become so much a part of the character of Christians in the last days it caused him to call our day *terrible times.*

This prophecy has come true in America. Christians have lost their power to overcome many of these worldly characteristics. We are no longer the people with clean hands and pure hearts with our affections set on things above. Divorce, immorality, dishonesty and greed run rampant in the church. We are no longer willing to sacrifice our self-interest lifestyle to seek God's standards first.

Paul ends this list of worldly characteristics he saw dominating Christians in our day saying, *having a form of godliness but denying its power.* Living the Christian life without the power of God is made evident if our character reflects these characteristics on Paul's list. The heart is what controls our actions. Not one of these characteristics on Paul's list is of God. If they control our nature it is because we have slowed, or stopped, the flow of the Holy Spirit as our power source in overcoming these worldly characteristics. How much and how often they are a part of our character reflects where we are spiritually.

To become Christ-like in the character of our heart is a key objective throughout the development of our Christian life. I will briefly describe the characteristics that controlled the heart of Jesus. They are the *true* character traits of Christianity. Satan is using the deceptive influence of society in any way he can to stunt and stop the development of these characteristics.

Jesus taught the general characteristics of a Christian in the greatest sermon ever preached, The Sermon on the Mount. Not one of these characteristics is fully obtainable over the lifetime of our spiritual development, but they should be what we set our eyes on and our commitment towards, as we grow spiritually. They are the mirrors by which we examine ourselves. These spiritual characteristics are the only formula for true happiness. Each one carries a promise or blessing of happiness. They help us see why so many people— Christians included—are unhappy, and are experiencing severe problems. Notice how different they are from the teachings of the world and opposite to those characteristics I quoted that Paul says will be common among Christians in the last days.

Christian Characteristic Number One: *Blessed* (happy) *are the poor in spirit, for theirs is the kingdom of heaven* (Matthew 5:3).

Jesus was poor in spirit. He was empty of any self-interest. It is the key to all that follows in the development of our Christian walk. This characteristic deals with the emptying of our self-will, our self-interest nature, our old sin nature, and being filled with God's nature through the power of His Holy Spirit.

This characteristic of Jesus is in direct conflict with all that is of this world. The world system promotes **self-assertion, self-satisfaction, self-exaltation,** and **self-glorification.** It emphasizes personalities, natural abilities, appearance, family heritage, nationality, natural temperaments, intelligence, wealth, worldly position and authority. The world system despises this quality of "poor in spirit" that was a foundational part of the teachings of Jesus.

All of the characteristics of Jesus listed in The Sermon on the Mount opposed practically every teaching you will find in the world. His character was such a direct conflict with the ways of the world the people of His day wanted to get rid of Him. They wanted Him out of their sight. They hated His character. They did not know how to deal with it. So they tried to shoot out the light of His character by crucifying Him. They did not know that you can't destroy the character of one's heart through death.

Don't try to use your own willpower to develop this characteristic of "poor in spirit." That is impossible. The same is true for any of these characteristics. We may try to change our personality by purposely bringing about some personal hardship or by removing ourselves from society. But this or any type of activity through our own strength will only end up making us less "poor in spirit" because that will create an even greater awareness of **self**. These Christian characteristics taught by Jesus can only be developed by the power of the Holy Spirit as we grow spiritually and allow Him to have greater control of our hearts.

Christian Characteristic Number Two: *Blessed* (happy) *are those who mourn, for they will be comforted* (Matthew 5:4).

This is another characteristic of the heart, which is totally contrary to the teachings of society. Jesus mourned because He saw the effects of sin on the human race and in the world as it really is. He did not try to escape from reality.

This characteristic of mourning is something most people run from. They try to avoid it altogether. It should hurt us deeply to see the way people are living in our society—their attitude towards the standards of God and the pain it is causing so many people. The world system is using an amazing amount of energy, enthusiasm and expense through worldly pleasure and entertainment to blind us to the effects of sin and to move us away from developing this "spirit of mourning." The degree to which we possess this characteristic plays heavily on our appreciation of the deep love God has for mankind and the commitment we will make to live the Christian life.

Jesus saw the harm this horrid, ugly and foul thing called sin did to the people. He saw its terrible results! It causes pain, sickness, grief, distress and unhappiness, in addition to sending people to the grave on their way to Hell.

What sin does to people is the reason Jesus mourned. He also knew that sin stabs God right in the heart. He knew how much pain sin has caused God. Not only for what it does to people but it was also the reason God had to send Jesus to suffer and die on the cross. It is the characteristic of mourning that will open our eyes to see the spiritual needs of mankind.

Christian Characteristic Number Three: *Blessed* (happy) *are the meek, for they will inherit the earth* (Matthew 5:5).

This is a characteristic of the heart that really brings us face to face with something completely opposite to the natural thinking of mankind.

For Jesus to say: *The meek shall inherit the earth,* baffled the wisdom of the world. Man's way of thinking is by relying on the strength and power of his military, material goods, intellect and aggressiveness to control and influence the world.

Jesus did not try to accomplish the things of God through man's ability. He submitted Himself and His will completely to God, being totally committed and dependent on Him and His power. Examples of people who developed this characteristic of meekness in their lives are: Moses, David, Abraham, the prophets, Paul, Peter, and I am sure there are many other godly men and women throughout the history of God's people that we never hear about.

Meekness does not mean to be flabby, lacking in strength, firmness, vigor or force. We can see that from the life of Jesus. He was not simply easy-going, nice, weak in personality, nor did He exhibit a compromising spirit of peace at any price. He knew His mission and set His face as a flint to accomplish it.

People talked about Him, scorned Him, stated untruths about Him, denied Him His rightful position, privileges, possessions and status in life, and did not allow Him the right to express His opinion.

But this characteristic of meekness caused Him <u>not</u> to demand His personal rights or position. He was a vessel for God to live in and work through. It was God's will and purpose He sought and lived for—not His own.

The apostle Paul demonstrated this characteristic of meekness, as he grew older. If he were alive today, he would probably hold a Ph.D. in philosophy and theology. He would have an understanding knowledge of economics, political science, history and the languages. He was a devoted religious man, zealous in his commitment to a religious system as a member of the Pharisee sect. By the standards of the world he had a long list of personal credentials.

But Paul lost all confidence in his credentials and natural abilities. He said: *I consider them rubbish, that I may gain Christ ...* (Philippians 3:8). That is what the characteristic of meekness means. It allowed God to accomplish more through Paul than anyone else in early church history. He wrote more books in the New Testament than anyone and his several missionary journeys became a part of Scripture.

We may not become a Moses, Paul, Peter or some other great spiritual leader. Even if that were God's purpose for us, it took the Lord many years to develop these godly characteristics in these individuals before they could completely accomplish the will of God in their lives. To fulfill God's will for our life we **first** must humble ourselves and surrender our will completely to the Lord. Only then can He develop in us the true nature of Jesus.

Christian Characteristic Number Four: *Blessed* (happy) *are those who hunger and thirst for righteousness, for they will be filled* (Matthew 5:6).

One of the major areas that distinguished Jesus from all other people is that He never sinned. He had a hunger and thirst for righteousness and He was filled.

To *hunger and thirst* is to have a deep and desperate need. It is the feeling one has if away from home for a long time and he or she is homesick. We become so desperate it hurts. To hunger and thirst for righteousness will develop in our heart an inner desire that desperately seeks the righteous nature of God. It will develop in us an attitude to examine all of our activities by biblical standards. This heart characteristic is what testifies of our commitment to obedience.

The promise of this characteristic is that we will be filled—not through our efforts, but through the power of God's grace. Jesus said: *But seek first his kingdom and his righteousness, and all these things will be given to you as well* (Matthew 6:33). Righteousness is the way to real peace.

Notice that Jesus did not hunger and thirst after happiness or blessings. He knew they are a natural consequence of seeking righteousness. If we seek after the wrong thing, the end result will be like a doctor treating the pain or symptom and ignoring the cause.

Christian Characteristic Number Five: *Blessed* (happy) *are the merciful, for they will be shown mercy* (Matthew 5:7).

The characteristic of mercy in Jesus is what allowed Him to see the miserable consequences of sin. It is what drove Him to act and relieve the suffering that sin causes mankind. Not only in this life but also in eternal life after we die.

It is mercy that allowed Jesus to see people with a different eye. It caused Him to have a deep sense of pity, compassion and sorrow for mankind and why He made the proper distinction between the sin and the sinner. He saw people as creatures that are slaves to sin on their way to Hell—creatures that need forgiveness—and mercy gave Him the desire to do something about it.

The characteristic of mercy develops a sacrificial love for mankind, a caring love that causes a person to do all he can to save another from the fiery pits of Hell.

I am so thankful we have a merciful God. He knows the consequences of sin. Mercy caused Him to have pity on mankind and take action to deliver us from being condemned. His characteristic of mercy not only saw the need, it caused Him to take action. He did something about the need. The Bible says: *For God so loved the world* (mankind) *that he gave his one and only Son* (Jesus Christ), *that whoever believes in him* (accepts Him in their heart as their Savior) *shall not perish* (spend eternity in Hell) *but have eternal life* (spend eternity in Heaven). *For God did not send his Son* (Jesus Christ) *into the world to condemn the world, but to save the world through him. Whoever believes in him* (accepts Jesus in their heart as their Savior) *is not condemned, but whoever does not believe stands condemned already because he has not believed in the name of God's one and only Son* (Jesus Christ) (John 3:16-18).

The Bible promises eternal life in Heaven to all that receive and remain faithful to Jesus Christ. *And this is the testimony: God has given us eternal life, and this life is in his Son. He who has the Son has life; he who does not have the Son of God does not have life. I write these things to you who believe in the name of the Son of God so that you may know that you have eternal life* (I John 5:11-13).

Mercy differentiates between the sinner and sin. God hates sin but loves the sinner. Mercy changes our attitude toward others. It causes us to begin to see people as creatures to be pitied—creatures that are slaves to sin—creatures that have been trapped and engulfed in Satan's world system who are suffering the awful consequences of sin.

After He had been beaten and was hanging on the cross being crucified, mercy moved Jesus to say: *Father, forgive them, for they do not know what they are doing* (Luke 23:34).

It was the characteristic of mercy that allowed Jesus to see through those who persecuted Him. He could see that they were victims of Satan and his world system.

Mercy and love for mankind is what drove Jesus to live the sinless life so He could fulfill His mission to be the perfect sacrifice for the sins of mankind and save us for eternal life. Our going to Heaven was far more important to Him than His own personal welfare.

Christian Characteristic Number Six: *Blessed* (happy) *are the pure in heart, for they will see God* (Matthew 5:8).

The single most important motivation behind all that Jesus did was to love, serve and glorify God rather than to serve Himself. He exemplified the characteristic of being *pure in heart.*

The whole foundation of the Christian doctrine, as lived and taught by Jesus, emphasizes having a *pure heart.* We need to be changed from the inside out and receive a new heart because by nature we do not have a *pure heart.*

This is the one characteristic that deals with all of mankind's problems. Jesus said: *For out of the heart come evil thoughts ...* (Matthew 15:19). Any problem or unworthy desire in life always stems from the heart.

To be *pure in heart* means freedom from hypocrisy. Hypocrisy may be the worst of all heart problems—because it is a lie within our heart that has an attractive cover to hide the truth. Hypocrisy is the cause of dishonesty, insincerity and it opens the door for us to be deceived.

A hypocritical heart will hide sin and its effects. It will only think of the pleasure and desire at the time. A *pure heart* is willing to reveal sin and the truth of its ultimate consequences.

The hypocrite may even claim to share in Christ and His righteousness. He might be involved in religious activity and even outdo the committed Christian. Judas confidently sat down with the apostles at the Passover as if he were the most welcome, holiest guest of all, yet his heart was evil and he eventually betrayed Christ.

We need to be sincere about our profession of Christianity. We must not speak about a personal relationship with Jesus Christ, when in our heart it is not true.

Job had a *pure heart*. Satan muddied up Job's life, but Job's spirit continued to flow from an honest heart before God. We need to be careful that we don't make a false profession of our spiritual state. To think and act like we are one place spiritually when actually we are in another place or really don't know, can be a very harmful deception of the heart.

David was called a *man after God's own heart* because in his heart there was no spirit of deceit. Yes, he was deceived and fell into sin, but there was no "spirit of deceit" which is to have a hypocritical heart. He had a *pure heart*! This is known because when his spiritual eyes were opened he quickly confessed and repented of the sin he had committed.

The key was the reaction of David's heart. He did not try to excuse or hide his sin. He knew he had done wrong and was ready for God's judgment. Because of his *purity of heart* David was quick to fully repent before the Lord and did not fall out of favor with God when he did wrong. Even though in this life he did have to suffer many terrible consequences because of the sins he had committed.

King David is a good example of the awful pain and heartache sin causes. Because of his repentant heart and confession before God, it did not keep him from spending eternal life in Heaven, but the pleasure of his sin for a short season brought him nothing but terrible misery for the last 20 years of his life on Earth.

To allow the Lord to develop a new *pure heart* in us is critical to our Christian walk. It brings a singleness of mind to seek God's holiness, His pure love, and a genuine faith that will truly reflect the evidence of Christ in our lives.

A *pure heart* is ready for spiritual responsibility because that heart is merged with God's will. Even when our best effort fails, the willingness of a *pure heart* means success to God.

Christian Characteristic Number Seven: *Blessed* (happy) *are the peacemakers, for they will be called sons of God* (Matthew 5:9).

Jesus had a mission to be a vessel that brought peace on Earth and goodwill to all men. What a beautiful characteristic it is to be a peacemaker! Of all aspirations in the history of mankind, whatever his endeavors, inner peace is the one thing that he strives the most to possess.

As a peacemaker Jesus was not a person who kept quiet just to avoid trouble or appease others all the time. It was this characteristic that caused Him to be absolutely neutral when surrounded by conflict and to be totally free from defensiveness and hypersensitivity. His sole interest was to bring inner peace to mankind regardless of the personal sacrifice required. He saw a larger, more important purpose in life than protecting His personal rights. That is why He went to the cross. It was to provide the hope of peace in our hearts.

As a peacemaker Jesus viewed all disputes, whether between individuals or nations, as distractions that detracted from the glory of God. He was selfless, loving and approachable. People could sense that He was a peacemaker and could approach Him knowing they would receive understanding and direction that would give them peace in their hearts.

The Character of a Christian

As a member of God's family these heart characteristics taught by Jesus are to become a part of our new nature. A careful look at the true characteristics of a Christian can be crushingly painful. However, it does help us to realize that only complete dependence on God will enable us to live our Christian life in a world that is so directly opposed to the characteristics of that life. What a contrast these Christian characteristics are to those taught and developed by the world.

Most of today's technology is used by Satan to keep our hearts closed to the truths of these heart characteristics. The powerful tools available in our society to teach and influence us to serve the cries of our natural desires is one of the major barriers we have to our spiritual growth because it is preventing the development and maturity of these true biblical Christian characteristics.

The influence of the American lifestyle goes to extreme measures to train the flesh (spoil it, so to speak) to get us to respond to the old nature. This condition of serving me, myself, and I makes it extremely difficult for us to take up our cross and deny self which is essential if we are going to fulfill God's plan of walking in the power of the Holy Spirit—the only power that can develop these characteristics Jesus taught.

We are seldom aware that we are walking in the characteristics of our old natural make up because it has become the norm. But it is made evident when we examine the fruits of our society and how little influence Christian standards now have on the way people live compared to the influence of the world. How we handle the everyday affairs of our life is the true reflection of our Christian character.

Who is wise and understanding among you? Let him show it by his good life, by deeds done in the humility that comes from wisdom. But if you harbor bitter envy and selfish ambition in your hearts, do not boast about it or deny the truth. Such "wisdom" does not come down from heaven but is earthly, unspiritual, of the devil. For where you have envy and selfish ambition, there you find disorder and every evil practice.

But the wisdom that comes from heaven is first of all pure; then peace loving, considerate, submissive, full of mercy and good fruit, impartial and sincere. Peacemakers who sow in peace raise a harvest of righteousness (James 3:13-18).

These general characteristics of a Christian taught by Christ tell us we do not control our Christianity. Our Christianity is to control us. *Being* is more important than *doing*.

Section Three
Preparing For God's Next Move

Chapter Eight

Separation

It may be difficult for some of you to handle all of the heavy issues I discuss in this book at one time. That is understandable! I do hope you will chew on what has been said, swallow what you can and put the rest on hold. Then as the Holy Spirit guides you, later take another look at the content of this message. The Holy Spirit must be our teacher. We are only the messengers.

America has become a culture that is heavily influencing Christians with the ways of the world. It has spiritually tainted most of us and even caused some Christians to fall away. The amount of spiritual harm the influence of our society has caused the body of Christ is difficult to evaluate. The fruits of our society, and the Christian community, compared to the teachings of Jesus Christ and the Word of God is not a pretty picture. The influence of the world's standards on God's people in our society has been much greater in this generation than the influence of the standards taught in the Word of God. The body of Christ in America has lost much of its light and the function of being salt—the preserver of good. This is reflected by how free people have become to openly talk about and display the most blatant of sins, flaunting them before the eyes of the public.

The Word of God tells us we are to be a separated people—

called out to live and reveal the holiness of God and His power so that we might save the people from the pain and anguish of their sins. But our light has been dimmed and our saltiness has lost much of its savor. We have become too much a part of the world and its ways. We mix the world's standards with God's standards.

Mixing With the World

The greatest hindrance in America that keeps Jesus Christ from becoming the power in our life, and giving us victory over our inner sin nature, is that Christians have become dependent upon and entrenched with the ways of the world. We are guilty of **mixing with the world.**

The word **mixture** means to combine or blend into one mass so that individual characteristics are gone. It is the intermingling of two elements, causing them to lose their separate uniqueness, and take on a new, singular character.

The influence of our modern electronic media has caused God's people to want to blend and intermingle. Our old sinful nature is naturally going to like many of the things of the world, but our mixture has caused us to lose our unique, different, special character. Our godly, righteous qualities have taken on many of the characteristics of the society in which we live.

God's warning is clear on the subject of the world, or what we today call society, and the harm it does to the Christian life. Here are a few of the many Scriptures that address this issue.

Do not conform any longer to the pattern of this <u>world</u>, but be transformed by the renewing of your mind. Then you will be *able to test and approve what God's will is* (that is a prom-ise)—*his good, pleasing and perfect will* (Romans 12:2).

Scripture teaches we are to keep ourselves unspotted from the world.

> *Religion that God our Father accepts as pure and faultless is this: to look after orphans and widows in their distress and to keep oneself from being polluted* (spotted) *by the <u>world</u>* (James 1:27).

God warns us to avoid friendship with society.

> *You adulterous people, don't you know that friendship with the <u>world</u> is hatred toward God? Anyone who chooses to be a friend of the <u>world</u> becomes an enemy of God* (James 4:4).

We are to be "in," but not "of" the world.

> Jesus said: *My prayer is not that you take them out of the <u>world</u> but that you protect them from the evil one* (Satan). *They are not of the <u>world</u>, even as I am not of it* (John 17:15,16).

We are not to love the world.

> *Do not love the <u>world</u> or anything in the <u>world</u>. If anyone loves the <u>world</u>, the love of the Father is not in him. For every-thing in the <u>world</u> ... comes not from the Father but from the <u>world</u>* (I John 2:15,16).

Why does the Lord give us such a strong warning against the world—what we call society? Because Satan is the god of society.

> *The god of this age* (world-society) *has blinded the minds of unbelievers ...* (II Corinthians 4:4).

Satan is the ruler of the kingdom of the air.

As for you, you were dead in your transgressions and sins, in which you used to live when you followed the ways of this <u>world</u> and the ruler of the kingdom of the air, the spirit who is now at work in those who are disobedient (Ephesians 2:1,2).

Society is under Satan's control!

We know that we are children of God, and that the whole <u>world</u> (society) *is under the control of the evil one* (that is Satan) (I John 5:19).

This is not to say Satan can rule over and above God's providence, but control of the world systems was given over to him. That is why to win our spiritual battles against Satan and the world system, the Bible teaches we are to prepare. We need the full armor of God. That has become especially true with the ability he has to teach through the electronic media in our culture!

Finally, be strong in the Lord and in his mighty power. Put on the full armor of God so that you can take your stand against the devil's schemes. For our struggle is not against flesh and blood, but against the rulers, against the authorities, against the powers of this dark <u>world</u> and against the spiritual forces of evil in the heavenly realms (Ephesians 6:10-12).

The world, or society, is Satan's **attack vehicle** in spiritual warfare. The Bible warns he is constantly at work using the world system to set his traps to entice and deceive Christians. In today's environment we seem to have difficulty in understanding that he runs **the world** order. We acknowledge that Satan has an *influence* in the world, but to admit that he *controls* society is difficult. I do <u>not</u> know all of the theological answers behind this issue of why he controls societies, but it appears from Scripture that control of the world order was handed to Satan when Adam and Eve fell. I know when Satan tempted Jesus, he told Jesus that all of the kingdoms of the world had been given to him and Jesus did not dispute Satan's position (see Luke 4:5,6).

That doesn't prevent us from taking something out of the world and converting it to be used for God's glory just as mankind is redeemed out of the world system. But there seems to be a constant temptation in our mind to reason against such a possibility that Satan controls the societies of the world. We have to trust God's Word on this truth.

Because we have a sinful nature we must be very cautious how we mix with the standards taught by society. Satan tempts the sinful nature—*the lust of the flesh, the lust of the eyes, and the pride of life*—with the things of society to cause us to no longer want to be a separated and different people.

From the very beginning, God chose to reveal His presence only through a special, separate people. He chose to reveal Himself through Israel—but only if they would avoid the **sin of mixture** with the world:

> *For you are a people holy to the Lord your God. The Lord your God has chosen you out of all the peoples on the face of the earth to be his people, his treasured possession* (Deuteronomy 7:6).

Moses knew there was only one thing that made them special, or different, from all other people on Earth. It was not because they were in themselves worthy or holy. It was the presence of God revealed in their midst! They alone had the actual presence of Almighty God!

The Lord replied, "My Presence will go with you, and I will give you rest." Then Moses said to him, "If your Presence does not go with us, do not send us up from here. How will anyone know that you are pleased with me and with your people unless you go with us? What else will distinguish me and your people from all the other people on the face of the earth?" (Exodus 33:14-16).

Here is conclusive proof that God's people are special and different because of the actual presence of the Lord in there midst! That is what walking in the power of the Holy Spirit means to a Christian. It is God's presence within that makes us different. Take away the power of His presence and our character is not much different than the rest of the world. We are not a separated people.

Any congregation or group of people can boast they are Spirit-filled, but if there is no overwhelming presence of Christ and victory over sin at work in their midst, they are just as ordinary as everyone else. Satan's modern day schemes to deceive have worked. We are unique only if Christ's presence is in full revelation among us. And that will be manifested by having victory over the power of our sinful nature and by overcoming the influences of the world in our lives.

God told Israel that any mixing with the world would cause Him to withdraw His presence, and He would reject them as the special channel of His revelation.

But Israel loved to mix! God's people were determined to do away with everything that made them different from the rest of the world. They despised the reproach of being separated. They wanted kings, like the rest of the world. They wanted wives from the world.

They wanted sexual freedom like the rest of the world. They wanted to flirt and indulge in adultery with the ways of the world and still cover the altar with tears. They wanted the lust, the passion, the immorality, the fornication and the idols of the rest of the world. So they rejected the Lord's commandment to be separated and special to Himself. They sinned and became proud and vain, and made themselves images and worshiped idols—to do evil in the sight of God as did the wicked.

> *So the Lord was very angry with Israel and removed them from his presence ... even Judah did not keep the commands of the Lord their God. They followed the practices Israel had introduced. Therefore the Lord rejected all the people of Israel; he afflicted them and gave them into the hands of plunderers, until he thrust them from his presence* (II Kings 17:18-20).

There was no need for Israel to seek after counselors or spiritual advisors or prophets to find out why they were so harassed and filled with despair. They knew why troubles were piling up on them—the presence of the Lord was gone!

The predominant message of the prophets was: *Your iniquities, or sins, have turned away the presence of God.* God spoke to His people through Jeremiah:

> *"Should you not fear me?" declares the Lord. "Should you not tremble in my presence? ... But these people have stubborn and rebellious hearts; ... Your sins have deprived you of good. Among my people are wicked men ... their houses are full of deceit; they have become rich and powerful ... they do not plead*

the case of the fatherless to win it, they do not defend the rights of the poor. ... Should I not avenge myself on such a nation as this? A horrible and shocking thing has happened in the land: The prophets prophesy (teachers teach) lies, the priests rule by their own authority, and my people love it this way. But what will you do in the end?" (Jeremiah 5:22-31).

Israel had mixed with the world around it, lost its unique character, and had taken on the character and identity of the world. So God hid His face from them, rejected their new character and withdrew His presence.

Have we missed a major point God is making in the Old Testament? How much clearer could it be? God will not put up with our mingling with the unholy, the unclean. Why was there such an emphasis on a separated priesthood in the Old Testament? To give us an example of God's firm commitment to reveal Himself only through a holy, clean, separated people.

> You and your sons are not to drink wine or other fermented drink whenever you go into the Tent of Meeting, or you will die. This is a lasting ordinance for the generations to come. You must distinguish between the holy and the profane, between the unclean and the clean, ... (Leviticus 10:9,10).

> You are to be holy to me because I, the Lord, am holy, and I have set you apart from the nations to be my own (Leviticus 20:26).

That is the special message of the Old Testament—the story of a unique severed, separated, different people who would maintain God's cause on the Earth, through a manifestation of His presence.

The New Testament is even stronger in condemning **the sin of mixing** with the standards of the world. There is nothing in the Old Testament quite as strong as the warnings of Paul against having an attachment with the world:

> *Do not be yoked together with unbelievers. For what do righteousness and wickedness have in common? Or what fellowship can light have with darkness? What harmony is there between Christ and Belial? What does a believer have in common with an unbeliever? What agreement is there between the temple of God and idols? For we are the temple of the living God. As God has said: "I will live with them and walk among them, and I will be their God and they will be my people." "Therefore come out from them and be separate, says the Lord. Touch no unclean thing, and I will receive you." "I will be a Father to you, and you will be my sons and daughters, says the Lord Almighty"* (II Corinthians 6:14-18).

A major requirement for walking in the fullness of God's presence—in the power of His Holy Spirit—is to no longer mix with the world and its standards. Satan knows that! Why do you think as his time is drawing short, he has used the influencing power of our society to attack the standards the majority of Americans have lived by? It is because we have been the heartland of Christianity and its teachings.

God wants the world to see the difference between His people who love Him and the rest of the unbelieving world. We are to be examples of a delivered and victorious people trusting in His mighty arm to deliver us from all harm and evil.

The reasons for separation from walking in the ways of the world are the same today as in the past. God draws a line between His people and the people of the world so that the unbeliever can know there is none like Him in all the Earth to deliver them. The wicked people of this age must have an even greater manifestation of the Lord's presence than in the past—nothing else will get their attention.

Whatever is mixed with the world is not of God. It can never be a channel of Christ's actual presence. Every confessed believer who yearns for the pleasures and seductions of this world is going to be exposed and left dry, empty and confused in the days to come. The Lord cannot—He *will* not—trust His holy presence to those that are not separated from the world in their hearts, and yielded only to Him.

Disobedient servants will not stand against the attacks of the devil, the moral landslide, the economic ruin and other chaotic conditions that are coming in this, the final years of the Gentile Age. They will once and for all lose the touch of God, and though some will be saved, they will be counted unworthy of the anointing. If you are of this world, you are not of His! Jesus said: *... I am not of this world* (John 8:23).

Speaking about His disciples, Jesus said: *They are not of the world, even as I am not of it* (John 17:16). *If you belonged to the world, it would love you as its own. As it is, you do not belong to the world, but I have chosen you out of this world. That is why the world hates you* (John 15:19).

Jesus is saying: *I have put a difference between you and the world. They will hate you because of the presence of my character in you.* People wanted to persecute Jesus because His nature was so different. His righteousness, illustrated in the characteristics I described from His Sermon on the Mount, made the righteousness of those around Him look cheap, second class, tasteless and showy. His light was so bright it showed up the darkness of evil in the hearts of men who did not want to believe they were evil. His light had to be extinguished, so they persecuted and killed Him.

If that is true, why are we trying to gain the approval of the world? Why do we seek their goodwill? Why do we bend our morals to accommodate them? Why do we seek their applause or blessing? We are not of this world! We need to accept this difference and quit trying to be like the people of the world if we are going to represent Jesus Christ and His teachings here on Earth.

The world loves its own—but we are not of it. May the Lord help us to joyfully accept His special holy character of separation and difference, and give up on the world. It will only be those who are truly separated unto Christ who will have any power to save the world. Jesus gave Himself that He might deliver us from this present evil world. How can we have any part of its standards?

Do not love the world or anything in the world. If anyone loves the world, the love of the Father is not in him (I John 2.15).

In a previous chapter I quoted Paul's comment about this! He said: *May I never boast except in the cross of our Lord Jesus Christ, through which <u>the world</u> has been crucified to me, and I to <u>the world</u>* (Galatians 6:14). To be crucified is to die or to be separated. Paul is talking about dying to the ways of the world.

The Holy Spirit will be calling out the true followers of Jesus Christ, separating them, purging them and getting them prepared as a special people to bring back His glorious presence to shake the Earth. We are going to be a people crucified to the world!

Most of us today are guilty to some degree of mixing too much with the world. We have been overcome by the power of the worldly influence in our society. John prophesies in Revelation 13:7 that the "beast" system would have the power to overcome the saints. Its power had an effect on my overall spiritual commitment—even though it was <u>not</u> my heart's desire to be spotted by the world. It seems nearly impossible for Christians to totally escape the deceptive influence of the "beast" society.

The Danger of Mixing With the World

In a previous chapter I discussed our **sinful nature**. It is made up of, *the lust of the eyes, the lust of the flesh, and the pride of life.* Everyone knows from their personal experiences in life that even though they are a Christian they still have the nature of a sinner within. As Paul explains there is *the law of sin at work within my members* (Romans 7:23). In our mind we don't want to be that way, but we didn't have a choice. Every human being is born with a nature to sin. This explains why God's Word warns against mixing with the world and its standards. To do so is treading on dangerous ground for a Christian. Because when we mix with the world our sinful nature is going to be tempted. We open the door for spiritual warfare.

A Christian should desire in his or her mind to do the will of God and follow His commands. But even the most sincere Christian knows how difficult that is at times. That is especially true in our society with the influence it has to teach us the self-centered ways of the world. The majority of Christians in America are self-centered.

We use the world's ways to fight for our rights, we get angry, are not patient and loving, get caught up in the things of the world, are not always truthful, loving, kind, selfless, devoid of pride, patient, obedient, longsuffering, and compassionate.

When the gospel of Jesus Christ <u>first</u> shined into our heart, our heart's cry was for *forgiveness*. But as we grow in our Christian walk we discover, as did Paul, that not only do we need forgiveness of our sins, there is something terribly wrong inside. The very same sin principle that plagued Paul within is at work within us as well. We need *forgiveness* for what we have done, but we also *need deliverance* from who we are—the power of the **sinful nature** rooted within our being that leads us to sin. Satan does all he can to prevent us from overcoming our sinful nature. His greatest tool in accomplishing this objective is the influence of the world coming from the things of society. His success is measured by how much fruit we bear for the Lord Jesus Christ and by how successful Satan is in keeping us from living victoriously over our sinful nature. That is why there are so many warnings in the Bible about our mixing with the standards of the world. It has tremendous power to tempt our sinful nature.

> *We know the law* (speaking of God's laws and commandments) *is spiritual; but I am unspiritual, sold as a slave to sin. I do not understand what I do. For what I want to do I do not do, but what I hate I do. And if I do what I do not want to do, I agree that the law is good. As it is, it is no longer I myself who do it, but it is sin living in me. I know that nothing good lives in me, that is, <u>in my sinful nature</u>. For I have the desire to do what is good, but I cannot carry it out. For what I do is not the good I want to do;*

no, the evil I do not want to do—this I keep on doing. Now if I do what I do not want to do, it is no longer I who do it, but it is sin living in me that does it.

So I find this law at work: When I want to do good, evil is right there with me. For in my inner being I delight in God's law; but I see another law at work in the members of my body, waging war against the law of my mind and making me a prisoner of the <u>law of sin</u> at work within my members. What a wretched man I am! Who will rescue me from this body of death? Thanks be to God—through Jesus Christ our Lord!

So then, I myself in my mind am a slave to God's law, but <u>in the sinful nature</u> a slave to the law of sin. (Although we are born with a sinful nature—something we must battle throughout this life—there is no condemnation for the mistakes we make if we are in Christ Jesus.)

Therefore, there is now no condemnation for those who are in Christ Jesus, because through Christ Jesus the law of the Spirit of life set me free from the law of sin and death. For what the law (all that is engrossed within God's laws and commandments) *was powerless to do in that it was <u>weakened by the sinful nature</u>, God did by sending his own Son in the likeness of sinful man to be a sin offering. And so he condemned sin in sinful man, in order that the righteous requirements of the law might be fully met in us, who do not live according to the sinful nature but according to the Spirit* (Romans 7:14-8:4). Read the balance of Paul's writing on this subject in Romans chapter eight.

The greatest spiritual warfare we have is between our sinful nature, which loves many of the ways of the world, and the true righteous nature of the Holy Spirit. They are both a part of our inner being after becoming a Christian.

The teaching about our need to be *delivered from the power of the old sinful nature* and how the enemy is using the things of the world to keep this from happening is not that prevalent in Christian circles today. Yet because our society has so much power to attract, tempt, and serve the nature of our flesh, it is a biblical message that is needed in the body of Christ.

Separation Reveals Commitment

Our desire should be to express the nature and characteristics of Jesus Christ in all we do. We are to be a holy and pure people, the salt of the Earth. *Do you not know that your body is a temple of the Holy Spirit, who is in you, whom you have received from God? You are not your own; you were bought at a price. Therefore honor God with your body* (I Corinthians 6:19). Many Christians act as though they do not believe this verse! We still act and think as though we belong to ourselves. We want to be independent! Our pride has made it tough for us to think we belong only to God to serve His purpose on this Earth.

I would not suggest that anyone attempt to change things through their own willpower. The battle is the Lord's. However, He wages His battles through His people. To do so, He needs a separated committed people. Seeing where we are in the realm of prophecy demands that all Christians consider their commitment.

The first question that needs to be answered when the subject of commitment is discussed in Christian circles is, "What exactly does it mean?" Our reaction normally centers on wanting to be involved in some activity. We want to place our confidence in something we can do through our self-willpower. We even go to extremes in carrying out tasks of a physical nature, making up rules and regulations, thinking that is what total commitment means.

Yet with all of our physical efforts it does not bring us true spiritual victory, which is to overcome our inner sinful nature and the self-centered ways of the world. We are still left longing for God's character of sacrificial love for mankind, His joy, abiding peace, patience, kindness, gentleness and self-control.

We do not experience victory because we try to understand and commit the activities of the flesh to that which is of a spiritual nature. Commitment to the Lord Jesus Christ must first be something of the Spirit—of the heart—not something of the flesh. For an activity to be the leading of the Holy Spirit it must follow a changed heart. The normal approach of using human wisdom and human understanding does not apply in the area of spiritual commitment. That which is of the flesh is flesh, and that which is of the Spirit is Spirit. We cannot combine the two (John 3:6).

To properly approach the subject of commitment we need to realize that God is a Spirit; therefore, what we commit first is to be of a spiritual nature. It is something that must come from our inner being. That was one of the key issues Jesus had to address with the Jewish leaders. They taught commitment to God was primarily wrapped up in physical activities. Jesus taught commitment must first come from the heart, then the proper activities will follow.

Recent history reveals that we have been repeating many of the same mistakes the Jewish people made by establishing a tradition of

interpretation that made keeping God's laws merely an external matter (Mark 7:1-15). When Jesus walked on this Earth He emphasized
the error of this false interpretation by the religious leaders. He was
clear in explaining that God looks at the heart—not merely the outward performance. Most Jewish leaders had developed from their
human wisdom an idea of what God was like; therefore, Satan was
able to deceive them with religious independence and spiritual pride.
They could not even recognize God when He came in the flesh in
the person of Jesus Christ.

We should learn this lesson well! The Jews knew the Scriptures
and they honored the name of God. They were zealous in wanting to
serve God, but it was by the wisdom of man. They were not willing to
commit—to sacrifice—their lives to the spirit of the law, which is to
the Lordship and character Jesus described in The Sermon on the
Mount.

We too often reject the total surrendered life because of indiffer-
ence to our spiritual needs. The influence of our culture has us too
busy pursuing worldly activities. We have become caught-up in the
treadmill of our daily existence. Our inner spiritual being has become
secondary. Like the Jews, we know many of the Scriptures intellectu-
ally and we honor the name of God. We are zealous in wanting to
serve, to be involved, but it is often by human wisdom and willpower.
The true Spirit of Christ and His glory becomes lost in our involvement because our heart is not really seeking to grow in the characteristics of Jesus. It is more concerned with satisfying our self-life.

Most of us don't really know to what degree we have become
attached to the things of the world or how to become unattached.
We aren't even sure this is necessary. The self-centered spirit of our

land and its influences have brainwashed us by continuously bombarding us with of the ways of the world. Our mind is now controlled most of the time through the continuous influence of the media—radio, television, movies, Internet, newspapers, magazines—as well as education. The power of this worldly influence has become so intense that most of us can't help but love, and be attached to some of the things of the world and its self-seeking ways. This plan of attack against Christians has happened, just as it was prophesied in the Bible, through the spiritual influence and direction of what John calls the "beast" system. It has caused us to become hearers of God's Word rather than doers. James warns: *Do not merely listen to the word, and so deceive yourselves. Do what it says. ...The man who looks intently into the perfect law* (God's Word) *that gives freedom, and continues to do this, not forgetting what he has heard, but doing it—he will be blessed in what he does* (James 1:22-25).

Commitment Versus Involvement

Commitment is the giving of ourselves—our total being—as a living sacrifice to God. It is a willingness to be changed—to be called out and separated from the ways of the world. Today, it seems *many Christians are involved, but few are committed.*

It is easy for us to be involved if we want to be! Most people consider involvement to be some activity. We can be active in our church or do many other works in the name of Jesus, but that does not mean we are committed to Him and His teachings. Commitment is when our activity is sacrificing all that is for our interest for the glory of God.

I appeal to you therefore, brethren, and beg of you in view of (all) the mercies of God, to make a decisive dedication of your bodies—presenting all your members and faculties—as a living sacrifice, holy (devoted, consecrated) and well pleasing to God, which is your reasonable (rational, intelligent) service and spiritual worship. Do not be conformed to this world—this age, fashioned after and adapted to its external, superficial customs. But be transformed (changed) by the [entire] renewal of your mind—by its new ideals and its new attitude—so that you may prove [for yourselves] what is the good and acceptable and perfect will of God, ... (Romans 12:1,2 Amplified Bible).

The giving of yourself as a living sacrifice for God to control is a fulfillment of the first commandment to love God with all of our heart, mind, body and soul. To love is to give: *For God so loved the world that he gave his one and only Son, ...* (John 3:16). He gave that which meant the most to Him. For us to love God is to give that which means the most to us—the giving of ourselves. It is the wholehearted desire to sacrifice our self-will to fulfill his will. That is what commitment is all about!

The Christian community in America, as a whole, is <u>not</u> presently a sacrificing body, but a self-seeking body similar to the church described in the Bible at Laodicea.

I know your deeds, that you are neither cold nor hot. I wish you were either one or the other! So, because you are lukewarm—neither hot nor cold—I am about to spit you out of my mouth. You say, 'I am rich; I have acquired wealth and do not need a thing.' But you do not realize that you are wretched, pitiful, poor, blind and naked. I counsel you to buy from me gold refined in the fire, so you can become rich; and white clothes to wear, so you can cover your shameful nakedness; and salve to put on your eyes, so you can see.

Those whom I love I rebuke and discipline. So be earnest, and repent. Here I am! I stand at the door and knock. If anyone hears my voice and opens the door, I will come in and eat with him, and he with me.

To him who overcomes, I will give the right to sit with me on my throne, just as I overcame and sat down with my Father on his throne. He who has an ear, let him hear what the Spirit says to the churches (Revelation 3:15-22).

Our commitment to activities, things, doctrines, ordinances, traditions, structures, and personalities has failed. It has not withstood the temptations that our enemy has thrown at us in our generation. As a result we have developed a self-willed, self-seeking lifestyle. Only a heart committed and sold out to Jesus can withstand the enemy's attacks coming through the power that our society has to tempt us. Only Jesus has the power to overcome the systems of the world. He said: *I have told you these things, so that in me you may have peace. In this world you will have trouble. But take heart! I have overcome the world* (John 16:33).

We need more of Jesus in our hearts! There is no other way to have the anointing of the Lord. We must decrease and the life of Jesus in us must increase. The Bible teaches that only Jesus can really change anyone. It is not religion, a church, or personal willpower. They might treat the symptoms—the outward aspects—but not the inner being. It is only when our character is changed on the inside that true spiritual victory is realized and the fruits of the Spirit become the normal Christian life. Only Jesus can set us free from our self-serving character. The enemy uses every available means through the power of the "beast" system in our society to prevent this from happening. Our mixing with the standards of the world and becoming attached to the things of the world inhibits our spiritual growth because it blocks the life of Christ within, which is the power we need to overcome our sinful nature.

Paul understood this spiritual principle. He had good reason to take pride in who he was in the natural man. He had religious training, political authority, economic status, educational background, and intellectual ability. Paul was totally involved. Yet when referring to his religious life he said:

> ... *If anyone else thinks he has reasons to put confidence in the flesh* (natural abilities), *I have more: ... But whatever was to my profit I now consider loss for the sake of Christ. What is more, I consider everything a loss compared to the surpassing greatness of knowing Christ Jesus my Lord, for whose sake I have lost all things. I consider them rubbish, that I may gain Christ and be found in him, not having a righteousness of my own that comes from the law, but that which is through faith in Christ—the righteousness that comes from God and is by faith. I want to know Christ and the power of his resurrection and the fellowship of sharing in his sufferings, becoming like him in his death, and so, somehow, to attain to the resurrection from the dead* (Philippians 3:4b-11).

Paul studied under one of the greatest philosophers of his day, Gamaliel. Paul was also very religious. He was a member of the Pharisee sect. He was involved.

Paul fasted a couple times a week, prayed three times a day, gave ten percent of his earnings, and I am sure he seldom missed attending the assembly. Paul had social status, born from the people of Israel in the tribe of Benjamin, and was able to trace his family heritage back to Abraham. Paul had good reason to take great personal pride in who he was. But he says: *All things which were gain to me, those I count lost for Christ; in fact I count everything loss that I might know Christ better.*

Paul's experience had taught him that there is only one power that has any force to deal with the influence and pressures of the world and its systems. It is Jesus Christ! A Christian's unqualified dependence is on Jesus Christ and Him alone. From start to finish, He is the one who does it all. Jesus Christ is everything and everything is in Him. In the matter of *forgiveness* we must look to Christ on the cross, in the matter of *deliverance* from the power of our inner sinful nature we must look to Christ in our hearts. For forgiveness, we depend on what He has done; for deliverance, we depend on what He will do within us. Both *forgiveness* and *deliverance* flow from the same source.

There is one single power that can deal with the influence and pressures of the world system. It is Jesus, only Jesus as He lives His life, in and through us, by the fullness of the Holy Spirit.

Even though the church is vital, a desire to commit completely to Jesus is not surrendering to a church or a church system of doctrine. Systems have been powerless to correct the spiritual defeat that is now plaguing so many Christians. Systems have not given Christians personal victory over their inner conflicts, emotional disturbances, poverty, hunger, hate, lack of brotherly affection and the sinful actions of the flesh. Systems have not given us victory over committing adultery with the world. Our church systems are not solving the breakdown of the biblical home structure. In fact it was recently reported that in America the divorce rate among Christians in the church is running about 8 percent **higher** than the divorce rate in the world.

A Christian commitment that does not require going to the cross to put to death our self-seeking lifestyle does not work. It does not bring victory. Our society is going backward in human relations rather than going forward because people are trying to live the Christian life without the power of Jesus Christ. Satan isn't too concerned with our Christianity if we keep making our own plans and running our own lives independent of a commitment to Jesus Christ. He, and He alone, is to be the center of our life, our commitment and worship. Paul said:

> *He is before all things, and in him all things hold together. And he is the head of the body, the church; he is the beginning and the firstborn from among the dead, so that in everything he might have the supremacy. For God was pleased to have all his fullness dwell in him, and through him to reconcile to himself all things, whether things on earth or things in heaven, by making peace through his blood, shed on the cross* (Colossians 1:17-20).

> *I have not stopped giving thanks for you, remembering you*

in my prayers. I keep asking that the God of our Lord Jesus Christ, the glorious Father, may give you the Spirit of wisdom and revelation, so that you may know him better. I pray also that the eyes of your heart may be enlightened in order that you may know the hope to which he has called you, ... (Ephesians 1:16-18).

I pray that out of his glorious riches he may strengthen you with power through his Spirit in your inner being, so that Christ may dwell in your hearts through faith. And I pray that you, being rooted and established in love, may have power, together with all the saints, to grasp how wide and long and high and deep is the love of Christ, and to know this love that surpasses knowledge—that you may be filled to the measure of all the fullness of God (Ephesians 3:16-19).

I have been crucified with Christ and I no longer live, but Christ lives in me. The life I live in the body, I live by faith in the Son of God, who loved me and gave himself for me (Galatians 2:20).

Paul had a revelation! There was only one way to overcome the power of his sinful nature within. It was in direct proportion to the degree of his relationship with Jesus Christ. Just as Jesus saved us from our sins, we are dependent on His power to *deliver* us from the power of the world system and the grasp of our inner nature that causes us to sin. Our dependence is in Christ alone. There is no other way! He must be the object of our Bible reading, study, and prayer. Our part is to have an open and honest heart with an attitude of repentance before the Lord like the young Christian man who shared his problem with addiction to pornography.

The self-seeking lifestyles that Christians have been influenced to develop in our culture has caused us to no longer want Christ as much as we want what He can do for us. We seek His healing power, His promises, His happiness, and more of this Earth's goods—but would we be satisfied with just Him alone?

David Wilkerson made an excellent comment on this issue. He wrote:

> *How many of us would serve Him if He offered nothing but Himself'? No healing, no success, no prosperity, no worldly bless-ings, no miracles, or signs and wonders.* **What If**—*once again we had to take joyfully the spoiling of our goods?* **What If**—*instead of clear sailing and problem-free living, we faced ship-wreck, fears within and fighting's without?* **What If**—*instead of painless living, we suffered cruel mocking, stoning, bloodshed, being sawn asunder?* **What If**—*instead of our beautiful homes and cars, we had to wander about in deserts in sheepskins, hid-ing in dens and caves?* **What If**—*instead of prosperity, we were destitute, afflicted, and tormented?*

The majority of Christians down through the centuries have lived their lives under these conditions. Review the early years of the church under Roman rule, the Dark Ages, and the Reformation wars. Study what is happening in countries today where, if you are a Christian, provisions of life are sacred. In these places Christians only have one thing. They have Jesus.

The only road to victory is our commitment to Jesus and all of

His teachings. There is such a limited amount of spiritual victory over the power of our sinful nature these days among Christians because we lack commitment to Jesus. We talk about Him, we sing to Him, wave our hands to Him, and these are good things, but would we be satisfied with only Him and nothing or no one else. *We once confessed our sins, but anymore it seems the majority of Christians in America are more concerned with confessing what they believe to be their rights.*

Our society is in chaos because we in the body of Christ are no longer a separated people surrendering ourselves to the fullness of Jesus Christ. We have lost our spiritual ointment to deliver our society from the power of sin that is hurting so many of its people. It's true! Look around. Many think Christianity is popular and that may be true in name, but we have lost our power. Our light is so dim we no longer bring conviction in the hearts of the people as very few seem to have a fear of sinning. Sin is openly displayed to the public on TV, radio, movies, magazines—you name it. The reason the world feels so free to do this is because Christians no longer seek first His righteousness, but seek first for their own benefits and position. So why shouldn't the world?

Commitment is to Sacrifice

Then he (Jesus) said to them all: "If anyone would come after me, he must deny himself and take up his cross daily and follow me. For whoever wants to save his life will lose it, but whoever loses his life for me will save it" (Luke 9:23,24).

Spiritual sacrifice is taking our self-life, our rights, to the cross.

We are to sacrifice our independence and our individualism. True commitment requires that the position of our physical nature be quite different than that which is common to man. We are a vehicle—a vessel for God to work in and through.

> *Therefore, my dear friends, as you have always obeyed— not only in my presence, but now much more in my absence— continue to work out your salvation with fear and trembling, for it is God who works in you to will and to act according to his good purpose. Do everything without complaining or arguing, so that you may become blameless and pure, children of God without fault in a crooked and depraved generation, in which you shine like stars in the universe as you hold out the word of life ...* (Philippians 2:12-16).

The spiritual power that separates us from the world and develops in us the characteristics Jesus taught in, The Sermon on the Mount, is the kind of purity the church needs.

The desire to sacrifice our self-life for the life of Christ is what God wants to see in our hearts. Giving up our independence and personal rights is not popular in Christian circles, but that is where the power lies. Only the true teaching of commitment to Jesus will develop those Christian characteristics that have the power to overcome our present world and its power.

It is Jesus Christ that develops our new character. *Therefore, if anyone is in Christ, he is a new creature; the old has gone away, the new has come* (II Corinthians 5:17). It is not religion, a church system or personal willpower. As previously stated these only change the symptoms, not the inner being of a man. It is only if our inner character is changed that true spiritual victory over the power of the world will be realized and the fruits of the Spirit become our normal Christian life. *But the fruit of the Spirit is love, joy, peace, patience, kindness, goodness, faithfulness, gentleness and self-control. Against such things there is no law* (Galatians 5:22,23).

Chapter Nine

Spiritual Surgery

Now for the painful lesson! Spiritual surgery is what it takes to heal the "spiritual heart disease" of *deception* and put to death our attachments to the world and our self-centered sinful nature. There is a spiritual principle taught in Scripture that says any part of my being that is controlled by me, can't be controlled by Jesus. Therefore, for Jesus Christ to control any part of our life, spiritual surgery must be performed to cut out, purge, and burn away that part of our self-life. The amount of spiritual surgery needed depends on the depth of my *deception* and how much I am attached to the things of the world.

Only God can perform this spiritual surgery. It is not within the power of man to change his inner nature. *The self will never crucify itself.* We may try by changing our physical state in life, but only God, or Satan, can work within the spiritual realm.

God knows our true being and what it will take to change our heart so that we will spiritually surrender our life to serve Him. He knows what we need to stand with the power of Christ to overcome the spiritual deceptions of the Evil One. Of course His spiritual surgery is never going to be completed. It is a never ending process, but our heart should be free enough of our old sin nature so we can be filled with enough of the life of Jesus Christ to carry out the functions of being His light and the preserver of His goodness and righteousness here on Earth. That is the salt this world needs and we once had in America.

Unfortunately the amount of spiritual surgery needed by the majority of Christians in America to make Jesus Christ the Lord of their life is going to require *serious* surgery. We live in such a powerful self-gratifying environment. The deceptive red herring Satan has devised through the power of our society to tempt the desires of our flesh has eroded the desire for a total committed life in most Christians. The influence of our society developed by the "beast" system has given our enemy so many weapons to teach its self-centered standards. Satan's objective to destroy America's Christian heritage has been very successful.

We Shall Be Held Accountable

When you consider all that Jesus has done for each of us in America and the over abundance of resources we have to be taught about Him, we are without excuse for our lack of commitment. That was my experience. I had no excuse! The Lord showed me I had been deceived because of my lack of obedience and commitment to follow His will. It had me on a path of falling away.

God's people have always been held accountable for the blessings they have received. The same is true of America. Human wisdom did not develop America. God has blessed our nation far above most countries throughout history. The history of our nation confirms that God has had a special place in His heart for America and the American people. We have been the world center of Christianity for over 300 years. God has used our people and our resources to take the gospel of Jesus Christ throughout the world.

Christians who were led by God to be salt and light settled our country. They did not let secular society form our government, although our government was designed to be secular—to be the government of all. Early Christians were involved in forming our Constitution, Bill of Rights, and every aspect of our Republic form of government. They were given wisdom and inspiration from God. No man had the wisdom and foresight that it took to build America.

It was the preaching of John and Charles Wesley, George Whitefield, David Brainerd, Jonathan Edwards and others in the 1700s during the Great Awakening revival that set the tone for our Constitution. Dr. Bill Bright states: *Fifty-two out of the fifty-five original signers of the Declaration of Independence confessed a personal relationship with Jesus Christ as their Lord and Savior.* Many of the original laws of our government were founded upon the teachings of the Bible. One of our founding fathers, John Adams, said it something like this: *Our Constitution is structured only for a moral and religious people.*

Between the years of 1800 and 1900, thousands of churches were established throughout our land. A church is found every few blocks in most towns across this nation, and the gospel is preached every day in our country through every communication media available. Until this generation, the standards that the majority of people have lived by in our country have been based on biblical teachings.

The Lord says: ... *From everyone who has been given much, much will be demanded; and from the one who has been entrusted with much, much more will be asked* (Luke 12:48). However, the moral fiber that bound our nation and our people together for centuries has unraveled. But that is not all, so have the moral standards of Christians. No longer are Christians the people with clean hands and pure hearts, with affections set on things above. No longer are we willing to sacrifice our self-interest life style to seek God's standards first. The moral structure of our society is collapsing, and we have done very little to stand firm and fight against the problem. Any Christian willing to face reality must admit that spiritually we are in serious trouble.

America has discarded the biblical standards on which our nation was founded as fast as yesterday's news. *If you can get away with it, then it is all right* has become the slogan of many people. Personal accountability, respect for authority, and self-control have become antiquated thinking. Nothing, it seems, is indecent or repugnant. Rules are not respected. Property of others is not respected. The unbelievable is permissible. Very little deserves to be honored.

We have sanctioned the murder of 40 million babies by abortion as an exercise in personal freedom. In reality this is the witness of a ghastly sacrifice of human life to the god of "self." Abortion should be an eye opening illustration of the self-serving spirit that has swept across our land in this last generation.

The church in America is not a committed—sold out—church to the teachings of Jesus. We are not full of righteousness, walking in the power of the Holy Spirit, overcoming sin. We are covetous, divorcing, depressed, worldly-minded, rebellious, grasping for materialism and success, competitive, lukewarm, permissive, adulterous, immoral, rich and increased with goods, unaware of spiritual blindness and poverty, pleasure-loving, filled with fear and anxiety, satisfied only to seek for good health and happiness.

What kind of church does Jesus deserve? An overcoming church! A people whose affections are set on things above! A people with clean hands and pure hearts! When I speak about the church, I refer to the overall state of the Christian community in our country. That is not to say there are none walking in victory over the power of the world system, but the majority are not.

These things are not said in a condemning way, or to show a critical spirit. But we need to be open and honest about the spiritual condition in our country. The power of the world has extinguished our light. In this generation we have become guilty of measuring spiritual progress by what we *know*, not by how we *live*. That is why the world began to shout: *God is dead!* No longer does the testimony of our lives bear witness that we are overcoming the influence of the world. We act and live and have the same personal problems as the people of the world.

We have shut out the presence of Christ in guiding our lives because we no longer want to be a separated people. We want to mix with the world and its standards. We no longer want to be different. Satan has caused the bride in our country to become adulterous with the world.

> *You adulterous people, don't you know that friendship with the world is hatred toward God? Anyone who chooses to be a friend of the world becomes an enemy of God* (James 4:4).

God disciplines people He has blessed if they allow *deception* to take root in their hearts and control their minds to the point where they become misguided and careless in their style of living a godly life. God's judgment or discipline is His way of correcting the elements that the enemy is using to keep us from serving, loving and following Him and His standards. Any judgment carried out by God is for our spiritual benefit. It is not for Him. It only brings pain to His heart. But it is His way of correcting those He loves. His love for us is far too great to let us continue on a path of spiritual destruction. ... *the Lord disciplines those he loves* ... (Hebrews 12:6). Discipline or judgment is God's way of performing His *spiritual surgery*.

We usually think of judgment as something negative, but when administered by a loving judge, judgment produces something for our good. A loving disciplinarian places the overall well being of the one in need of correction above personal feelings and the inner hurt and pain experienced by carrying out the discipline. Uncompromising discipline and sacrificial love go hand in hand.

Several Christian leaders in our country have said that America is racing toward God's judgment—Dr. Billy Graham, David Wilkerson, Dr. Henry Blackaby, James Robinson, Pat Robertson, Larry Burkett, Bill McCartney, to name a few.

We have become wrapped-up in our self-seeking pursuits and careless living in our country and this has led us into great danger—an overall lack of respect for the standards of God. This was a major aspect of spiritual deterioration in Noah's day, and according to Scripture it is of great concern to God today. It brought down God's judgment in the past and as we examine some of the things that have happened in our country it is becoming more and more apparent that the many ills we are experiencing in our society are signs that God is lifting His hedge of protection from America.

· **The family, the most fundamental means of preserving**

social order, has been shattered.

· Greed and unethical conduct have tainted professions (doctors, bankers, lawyers, politicians, educators, some spiritual leaders, etc.) that have historically represented the "pillars of society."

· Crime and violence stalk America's great cities, once the principle evidence of a mighty, industrial nation.

· Sexual immorality and life styles devoted to self-gratification have transformed the American character.

· Public schools, once the showpiece of a young democracy, have surrendered to drug abuse, sex, and criminal violence.

· Our government has turned its back on the scriptural principles that formed the moral foundation of this nation.

· Americans have reserved their most vicious attack for children through abortion and child abuse.

The rotten fruit produced by our society is there for all to see, and Jesus said that we could know the health of a plant by looking at its fruit. There is no excuse for any Christian to be uninformed. We cannot afford to put our heads in the sand. Things are going to get worse. Yet, as it was in the days of Noah, many are too caught up in the everyday affairs of life to hear and believe that God's judgments have begun.

A Time of Testing

A time of testing is coming. The Lord is going to shake, scrub, purge and purify the body of Christ in America. He will take the worldly dross out of us. All sin, adultery, and foolishness will be exposed.

If God's judgments are even a possibility, you should have some understanding of how to prepare yourself to survive these last days with the least amount of trauma. It is important to be ready for whatever the Lord's next move in America is going to be. According to the biblical teachings I have studied I am of the opinion most of us are not ready for what is coming. Jesus said:

> *Those whom I love I rebuke and discipline. So be earnest and repent. To him who overcomes, I will give the right to sit with me on my throne, just as I overcame and sat down with my Father on his throne* (Revelation 3:19&21).

Through a time of discipline and purifying, God is going to let the devil and the world know who has the power. It will develop a heavenly vision of holiness and humility in us. No longer will we want to hold on to our worldly vision that has been developed by Satan's deceitful schemes.

The time of testing that is coming will demand that we come to know the Lord in all of His fullness and glory, with our eyes focused on eternal values. Our false values will tumble and earthly dreams and plans will lose their meaning. We will be refined as gold and become the committed bride that Jesus deserves in these last days. The Holy Spirit is going to woo the children of the Lord away from the bigness, brightness and sensationalism. He is going to revive and sanctify His people to discern between the clean and unclean.

The next major event to occur in America will probably be the collapse of our materialistic economic system. The economic spirit of Babylon has taken over our country. Our pride is so strong we have become self-sufficient and independent wanting to solve our own problems and build our own arrangement of things. It has drawn the body of Christ into the enemy's trap of mixing with the world. We have become a part of the self-centered "great society" theme that is promoted in America, which is an expression of the religion of humanism.

How could our economic power collapse? I am not sure! But I can see that our economic structure is at a boiling point. Professional economists across the land agree it could explode at anytime. As a nation, we cannot continue to build up the huge deficits we now have so people can live in luxury. Our greed for things and our self-seeking lifestyle has driven us deeply into debt. Serious debt! People face huge personal debt. Corporations juggle massive business debt. Government operates with huge deficits. It should be noted that some economists differ as to whether government debt is truly hurtful to our economic viability since the U.S., based on current appraised value, has far more in assets than debt. But there is no major difference of opinion on the hurtfulness of consumer debt.

I will take a look at our consumer indebtedness—it is closer to home. Outstanding consumer debt—not counting real estate—in our country was $296 billion dollars in 1982. It is now close to $1.5 trillion. That is five times higher than what it was just a few years ago. And that number does not include real estate debt. Total consumer installment debt, such as credit cards, now outstrips total income for the first time in history.

The average amount owed on each and every credit card in our country is reported to be around $5,000.00. That is the average, and many Americans have more than one credit card! The total owed on credit cards by the American people is reported to be about $400 billion dollars and we pay approximately $80 billion dollars per year of interest on these credit cards.

For many American families it now requires two incomes to meet debt obligations. The loss of one income, even for a brief period, could put them dangerously close to financial ruin. Overall personal bankruptcies, individuals who have gone bankrupt, have climbed from 300,000 per year in 1980 to 1.4 million per year in 1997. This statistic is so alarming because we are living in a so-called period of prosperity! Our economy is currently in a boom, not a recession. Imagine what will happen if the economy weakens. Needless to say, millions of Americans will be in serious financial trouble if we experience a decline in the economy. The "spirit of merchandising" has overwhelmed the hearts of most American people.

Many economists believe the indebtedness of the U.S. economy has reached the point of no return and may be irreversible. It would be convenient to ignore this, but the consequences of our nation's reversal of fortune since the 1940s are inescapable. During the 1980s, our country shifted from being *the largest creditor* nation in the world to *the largest debtor* nation. The benchmark for our standard of living became so high the only way to finance our expectations was to borrow. Buying on credit became the only way for many Americans to get what they need—or are enticed by the world-system to want. Few seem to understand the reality of our country's economic position vis-a-vis the rest of the world. *We have mortgaged the future to pay for the present without counting the cost.* We have fallen into heavy debt. Personal debt has reached a record high. Savings an all-time low! The world's trap set by the materialistic influence in our society has worked! It has caused the body of Christ to commit adultery with the world and God is going to allow that economic bubble to burst. That is one of the surgical procedures He is going to perform spiritually as he burns out of His people their attachment to the world.

When will an economic downturn happen? No one, except the Lord, knows for sure! But when it does take place it will shake the world because the whole world is dependent on our economy. It will be sudden and quick! The people in the world will be without warning other than the voices of those Christians that God has chosen to speak through.

There were Christian ministries who thought we might experience troublesome times because of a Y2K computer problem. Of course that didn't happen, but I certainly don't question those who prepared. They have gained a tremendous amount of understanding on the subject of preparation. It is quite possible the body of Christ may look back and be very thankful that some of God's people are trained and knowledgeable to help when the economic bubble does burst. It may be that their motivation to prepare was an act of God's love and mercy towards mankind that will be used later.

This could be a great opportunity for the body of Christ to evangelize and meet the needs of people if Christians are spiritually, as well as physically, prepared. However, the availability of so many things of the world in our society, and the fact that credit is so easily obtained, has made it extremely difficult for most Christians to seriously take to heart any form of preparation.

At some point the Lord is going to take us out of being so heavily influenced by the worldly standards of our society. His purging, shaking, scrubbing and burning that we need is going to change our present conquered spiritual condition. We will be the better for it, because the purging of the Lord will cause us to become more dependent on only Jesus Christ. It will dissolve the attachment of our heart to the things of the world. It will usher in the revival that Christians in our country have been praying for!

How long will it take for the Lord to accomplish His task of breaking our attachments to the things of the world? Only the Lord knows the amount of *spiritual surgery* required. It is all in the hands of God. Praise His Holy Name that we can trust Him and His love.

> *Endure hardship as discipline; God is treating you as sons. For what son is not disciplined by his father?* (Hebrews 12:7).

> *... but God disciplines us for our good, that we may share in his holiness. No discipline seems pleasant at the time, but painful. Later on, however, it produces a harvest of righteousness and peace for those who have been trained by it* (Hebrews 12:10,11).

> *... God has said, "Never will I leave you; never will I forsake you." So say with confidence, "The Lord is my helper, I will not be afraid. What can man do to me?"* (Hebrews 13: 5,6).

FEAR NOT THE DAYS TO COME, BUT FEAR THIS ONLY: THAT YOU SHALL WALK IN A MANNER PLEASING TO THE LORD.

The following was written by a sister in the Lord and given to my brother, Bob Fraley. It is a word of encouragement to those who will put their trust in the Lord.

Darkness will soon cover the Earth; the ocean waters quiver with the oncoming storm. Many ships will drift aimlessly in the troubled waters; many will appear secure and sturdy, but they will be following a false light and the wrong direction. Do not chart your course by ships on your left or your right—look only to me (Jesus) for your direction. Many will follow the assuredness of those ill-fated ships, but they will meet with the same destiny.

Your ship will be tossed, rocked and battered by the wind and rains, but I will be with you in the same manner as I was with my apostles—ready to command your rough seas to "Be still!"

Just as in the days of Noah did I make my plans known, so I am doing now also. Only I can tell you how to build your ark ... only I can tell you what provisions need to be taken aboard for your survival. Others would say to you, "this is your need," or "that is your need," but I alone know your true needs: And when the storm begins, your safety and comfort will come in knowing that I am in control of your life.

Many bright beacons will tempt your path with "here, over here you will find quiet waters!" Or "this is your way to safety!" But do not be deceived, these beacons would lead you astray.

The hand of the Living God has set your course—stand firm and do not waver. Be not moved by what goes on around you, but affix your eyes on me and do not remove them. Trust in my ways, and cast your fears to the wind. I will never leave you nor forsake you.

The fruits of most Christians in America reveal that we are not prepared for God's warning about our over commitment to the everyday affairs of life that have strangled many of us. We are not prepared to handle God's warning of seducing spirits that have deceived our hearts into accepting many of the world's standards. We are not prepared for God's warning about the lawless spirit that would explode across the central area of Christianity in the last days. We are not prepared for God's warning about how all of this would cause worldly characteristics to become commonplace in the lives of many Christians.

Spiritual preparation was the key to Noah's success during God's judgment in his day; it was the key to those in Israel who saw their needs met when God had to judge Israel; and it will be the key to our success as God's judgments increase in America. It has been that way since the beginning of mankind. The Lord has always been faithful to meet the needs of those who are faithfully following Him and His ways. We need to develop a strong spiritual foundation now!

If our day is similar to the days of Noah, which the Bible says they are (Luke 17:26-28), then a good source for gaining information about spiritually preparing for God's judgment is to review the attitude and activities of Noah. Hebrews 11:7 gives insights about Noah that will help us know how to prepare. It says:

> *By faith Noah, when warned about things not yet seen, in holy fear built an ark to save his family. ...* (Hebrews 11:7).

The **first** thing that caused Noah to prepare himself and his family was **his faith**. He believed God's warning! That must come first or we will <u>not</u> seriously prepare ourselves for these last days. Before anything else, we must *believe* the signs of the time. We must first believe that God is trying to show us that His judgment hand is beginning to fall. Otherwise we won't be open to accept direction from God and His Word about what to do to prepare ourselves.

In His mercy God is allowing His judgments to begin slowly that we might wake up! That we might believe! All things in our relationship with the Lord begin with our faith. The same truth applies in this situation. If we can't see and believe that His judgments have been released on our nation with what has happened in this generation, chances are we won't be willing to step out in faith to follow the Lord's leading in how we should prepare.

Unfortunately it often takes a crisis before people will believe, regardless what the issue may be. In the past separation from the ways of the world only came about in God's people through a time of testing by God's judgments. That is how the Lord had to deal with the nation of Israel to get their attention and it was recorded in Scripture to be an example for us.

The **second** important thing we learn about Noah's preparation is his **attitude**. After receiving a warning from God, which he believed, he stepped out in faith with an attitude of *holy fear* within his character and took action. This is critical! Holy fear is what motivates humans to adhere to God's standards and not give in to worldly standards. Godly moral standards had been lost in Noah's day. But possessing a holy fear of God in his character, Noah cultivated a deep reliance on God and a love for God's standards. Hebrews 11:7 says of Noah: *... in holy fear built an ark to save his family.*

Walking in holy fear led him to take action to save his family. He trusted in God and His Word completely. His obedience was foremost in his mind because he had a proper fear or respect for the Lord.

Since our times are similar to Noah's, it will be this same attitude that will help preserve us. A few of the many verses that touch on the subject of having a proper fear of the Lord are:

> ... *learn to fear the Lord your God* ... (Deuteronomy 31:12). *The Lord confides in those who fear him; ...* (Psalm 25:14). *Let all the earth fear the Lord ...* (Psalm 33:8). *The angel of the Lord encamps around those who fear him, and He delivers them* (Psalm 34:7). *To fear the Lord is to hate evil; ...* (Proverbs 8:13). ... *through the fear of the Lord a man avoids evil* (Proverbs 16:6). *Then the church ... was strengthened; and encouraged by the Holy Spirit ... living in the fear of the Lord* (Acts 9:31). ... *live your lives as strangers here in reverent fear* (I Peter 1:17).

To have a holy fear is to stand in awe of and have a deep respect for God's holiness and His standards. Possession of this characteristic is what gives us that inner desire to avoid sin in our lives in every way that we know. It gives us a conscious desire to avoid anything we are aware of that would displease the Lord. Obedience becomes our utmost priority.

To have a proper holy fear of the Lord means to seek His will in all things—to examine every aspect of what is going on in our life with God's Word. Concern about *not* being in God's will, will be the driving force behind every thought and action.

Holy fear develops the desire to subject everything in our lives to the same exacting standard: *Is this pleasing to God?* Holy fear develops a heart that is pure, open to conviction and repentance. It allows the Lord to open our spiritual eyes. Holy fear gives us *discernment*.

To keep in line spiritually, a Christian needs to have a proper fear of the Lord. If we don't have a proper holy fear, we will take certain spiritual things for granted. We lose our sensitivity and alertness to the influence of the world around us. We easily develop spiritual pride and take liberties, which not only affects our spiritual walk, but also will hurt others. Without a holy fear of the Lord our heart can quickly become hypocritical in areas. We don't have a fear of sinning like we should. We become negligent in seeking His righteousness.

Holy fear is needed for a healthy spiritual walk. Jesus always kept His eyes on the mark. He avoided sin at every turn. He never wavered. A proper holy fear will help keep us from falling away from God's standards towards worldly standards. It will help us <u>not</u> to easily be led astray by those who have gotten off the track.

To spiritually **be prepared** for the judgments that we see are beginning to take place in our society, and for those that will become more severe, will require no less on our part than it did on Noah's part. By faith he believed God and moved with a holy fear to prepare an ark to save his family. A healthy, fearful attitude toward God is a key for you to have the wisdom in knowing how to properly prepare for His coming judgments.

If your standards as a Christian allow you to walk along the edge of darkness, then it is a sure indication you don't have the kind of holy fear towards God that Noah had and that Scripture talks about. It is important that we stay as far away as possible from worldly standards and give no advantage to Satan as we prepare ourselves spiritually. Our habit of mind must be to have a strong desire to avoid sin at every turn, to walk uprightly in a manner pleasing to Him, and to live in awe of the Lord. That is what it will take to build the ark we need to keep us safe from the pressures, temptations, and trials of our day as the battles become more severe and more often.

The severity of God's judgments waits around the corner. We should act now upon what we learn from Noah. Those who fear the Lord have nothing to be afraid of from the world in the days to come no matter what happens. That is because great courage against the enemy begins with a proper fear of the Lord. According to Scripture, the Lord will protect us regardless of circumstances if we have a healthy fear of the Lord.

In addition to Hebrews 11:7 there are other areas of Scripture I suggest you seek out and study that give insights about being under God's judgment—Isaiah chapters 1 through 5 for example. I will not review those chapters in this book, however, they are examined in an article written by my brother, Bob Fraley, titled *God's Coming Judgment*. This article is available from Christian Life Outreach. Their address is at the end of this book.

There is one other Scripture about preparing for judgment that I do want to review. It is II Chronicles 7:13-14. Verse 14 is often quoted these days but I like to also include verse 13 because these two verses go together in Scripture to make one sentence. They say:

> *When I shut up the heavens so that there is no rain, or command locusts to devour the land or send a plague among my people, if my people, who are called by my name, will humble themselves and pray and seek my face and turn from their wicked ways, then will I hear from heaven and will forgive their sin and will heal their land (II Chronicles 7:13,14).*

The setting behind these two verses is interesting. They came as a Word from God through Solomon for the Israelites during a time of great prosperity. At the time Israel was not under judgment. Their prosperous conditions were similar to those in America as I write this book. America is currently experiencing a time of great prosperity.

The *first part* of II Chronicles 7:13 and 14 definitely speaks of being under God's judgment. Then the *second part* informs the people of the things they must do when they come under God's judgment. The Word of God does not change. We need to learn these principles.

If my people who are called by my name definitely directs verse 14 to God's people which today are Christians. It is important to see the Lord's direction during a time of judgment is prefaced with the word *if*. There are conditions we must follow before the promise at the end of this verse will be fulfilled.

The **first** *if* condition is *will humble themselves*. We might do the other things mentioned in this verse—pray, seek God's face, and even turn from our wicked ways—but until we learn the lesson to humble ourselves, it does not appear the Lord will lift His hand of disciplinary judgment. You may recall humility or meekness was one of the key heart characteristics that Jesus emphasized in The Sermon on the Mount.

A strong purpose of God in bringing judgment upon a person or a nation is to humble them or deal with the pride in their hearts.

The **second** *if* condition in II Chronicles 7:14 is to *pray*. The **third** is to *seek God's face*. This is primarily done through the study of His Word. There is a lot of material available about prayer and seeking God's face. I would suggest every Christian be involved in a good Bible study on both. One study I would recommend on **seeking God's**

face is *Experiencing God* by Henry T. Blackaby & Claude V. King.

The **fourth** *if* condition was to *turn from their wicked ways.* To *turn from* means to repent. *Their wicked ways* would mean God's people must turn from following the ways of the world and seek His righteousness.

This message in II Chronicles 7:14 was to believers, not to the people of the world. I need to emphasize that in a time of judgment the Lord is trying to break and separate His people from their attachment to the world and its standards. There are several things the Lord says we must do to spiritually get our lives back on the right path. We are **to humble ourselves, pray, seek God's face, repent, and seek God's righteousness.** *If* we will do these things, He says: *...then will I hear from heaven* (hear our prayers) *and will forgive their sin and will heal their land* (bring revival).

For revival to take place all of these "if" conditions are to become a part of our Christian life. This principle applies to an individual, a church, and to a nation.

God's formula for you and me to prepare ourselves for the days ahead is: First, we must believe God's warning through the signs of the time that greater judgments are going to fall! We are to move with a holy fear in our hearts to build an ark of protection, which today would primarily be a spiritual ark. We are to follow His instructions of building this spiritual ark by humbling ourselves (swallowing our pride and become dependent on the Lord in all things), praying, seeking His face (spending time in His Word), repenting, and seeking His righteousness, all for the purpose that we may personally experience a revival in our heart. These are the necessary ingredients to build a spiritual ark of protection before the Lord. *If we do these things we will* **be prepared**. We will be able to hear from the Lord and know what His will is—His good, pleasing and perfect will.

A Word from the Lord for those who are willing to make the proper preparations states:

> *In righteousness you will be established: Tyranny will be far from you; you will have nothing to fear. Terror will be far removed; it will not come near you. If anyone does attack you, it will not be my doing; whoever attacks you will surrender to you. "See, it is I who created the blacksmith who fans the coals into flame and forges a weapon fit for its work. And it is I who have created the destroyer to work havoc; no weapon forged against you will prevail, and you will refute every tongue that accuses you. This is the heritage of the servants of the Lord, and this is their vindication from me," declares the Lord* (Isaiah 54:14-17).

Chapter Ten

A Final Word

You may have read this book and are not sure that you are a true born again Christian. True biblical Christianity is not following a religion. It is based on one thing—the gospel of Jesus Christ and the teachings of the Bible. *Yet to all who received him* (speaking of Jesus Christ), *to those who believed in his name, he gave the right to become children of God—children born not of natural descent, nor of human decision or a husband's will, but born of God* (John 1:12,13).

Jesus was actually God Himself come to Earth in the flesh. His ministry only lasted for about three and one-half years. Yet the effect of His life on the history of mankind has been unbelievable. It is far greater than anyone who ever lived.

He lived in poverty and was reared in obscurity. He received no formal education and never possessed wealth or widespread influence. He never traveled extensively. He only once crossed the boundary of the country in which He lived. In infancy He startled a king; in childhood He puzzled doctors; in manhood He ruled the course of nature, walked upon water, spoke and the sea was calm, raised the dead, healed the sick and made the blind man to see.

He never wrote a book. Yet His life has inspired more books

than any other man. He never wrote a song. Yet He has furnished the theme for more songs than all the songwriters combined. He never marshalled an army, nor drafted a soldier, nor fired a gun. Yet no leader has ever had more rebels surrender to Him without a shot fired.

The names of great statesmen have come and gone. Scientists, philosophers, and theologians are soon forgotten. But the name of Jesus Christ abounds more and more. Once each week the wheels of commerce cease their turning, and multitudes gather to pay homage and respect to Him.

His enemies could not destroy Him, and the grave could not hold Him. He was God on Earth in the form of a human being. If you want to know God, which I trust you do, look at the life of Jesus Christ.

Many people think it is difficult to become a Christian. They think they are not good enough or could never be good enough. That kind of thinking is incorrect. It is based upon something other than true biblical Christianity and what God has done for mankind. You need to erase that idea from your mind. True biblical Christianity is not difficult! God has made it very simple. It is man who has made it difficult.

We may not understand all that happens when a person has a personal encounter with Jesus Christ as their Savior and Lord. But if we truly ask Him into our heart we experience what is called *a spiritual rebirth—being born again*. It is something that is real and far beyond some exercise of the imagination.

You Are Something Special to God

You may not understand how you could be something special to God, and you may not feel that way when you look at all that has happened in your life. However, every person born is something special to God because He created man in His very own image. *So God created man in his own image, in the image of God he created him; male and female he created them* (Genesis 1:27). Mankind is a special product out of a special deliberation of God. That makes each one special in His eyes. That is why God's plan of salvation is available to anyone regardless of what they may have done in their past.

Humans are special, unique, and deeply different from all other of God's earthly creatures. There is never a hint anywhere in the Bible that being created in the image of God applies to any other form of life on Earth—any animal life. That is why God gave mankind dominion over all the other creatures. There are some similarities in our physical make-up with animals, but we are not the same in our spiritual make-up. That completely distinguishes mankind from all other creatures.

Mankind has intellect and a reasoning power far above all mere animal instinct and intuition. Animals cannot reason beyond instinct. The human intellect can reason, know, and grasp realities beyond Earth, time, and sense; and can contemplate the spiritual, eternal, divine.

Humans have a moral consciousness. We are a God-conscious being. We can know God, respond to Him, and commune with Him. The most exhaustive animal psychology has never found the faintest hint of either moral awareness or awareness of a Supreme Being in animals. Our nature is definitely different from that of animals.

Our modern day computer technology makes animal life appear as though animals have reasoning power, intellect and a conscious—even talk—**but that is make believe.** It is not real life! That is Hollywood. It is entertaining but be cautious. It is a false presentation of God's creation. Don't allow it to affect your thinking to the truth of God's real creation. Mankind is uniquely made in the image of God. We are special to Him above all other things in His creation. So special that even if we have been rotten to the core in our actions He literally had His Son, Jesus Christ, die for us so we could spend eternity with Him in Heaven.

All true born again children of God will spend eternity in Heaven, a special place that is more valuable than gold, silver, diamonds or anything else known to mankind. Jesus said the salvation of one soul, so they would go to Heaven rather than Hell, is worth more than the value of the whole world. Choosing Jesus Christ to save us is literally the difference in our choosing the value of Heaven over Hell. It is the most critical decision anyone ever makes in this life.

God has done His part to save all mankind. It is up to us to choose if we want to accept or reject His plan. That is another part of God's great love for His creation. He did not create us as robots. He created us with a free will. <u>He allows us to choose</u> where we will spend eternity. It is a decision everyone must make. There are no options. We choose either Heaven or Hell. In fact, if we ignore the subject or don't want to think about it, which is what a lot of people do, in reality they are making a choice.

You do not want to *miss* Heaven and God does not want you to *miss* Heaven. This beautiful place called Heaven is a free gift from God to mankind. Our mental state in Heaven will be so superior to anything known on Earth, words cannot describe it. Our capacities will be unlimited, supernatural. Our energy boundless! Our years never age. We never hunger or thirst, experience any pain, fear, doubt, defeat, regret, stain, misunderstanding, sorrow, temptation, sickness, stress, and on and on.

Everyone in Heaven lives in complete love, peace, joy, and happiness with beautiful surroundings as all provisions are provided by a loving God who created mankind and is now caring for all of those who love Him. This condition will never change. It will last for eternity—forever. It will never end.

You may have already heard what I am talking about but are not sure it is what you believe. You may be thinking that even if it is true I could never be good enough to pass the test so why try. That is a common thought. And you are correct if you think you can't be good enough to secure a place in Heaven. No one has ever been good enough, not even the great men of God in the Bible. However, that is another part of God's great love for His creation. He knows your thoughts. He knows they are true to you. He knows we have a sinful nature, which I discussed earlier in this book

That is why God has made the condition for securing a place in Heaven simple. In fact so simple it seems most people pass right over it. That is because mankind, through man made conditions, has made it difficult, not God. This is the Good News of the Gospel of Jesus Christ and why when Jesus was born the angels in Heaven were praising God.

And there were shepherds living out in the fields nearby, keeping watch over their flocks at night. An angel of the Lord

appeared to them, and the glory of the Lord shone around them, and they were terrified. But the angel said to them, "Do not be afraid, I bring you good news of great joy that will be for all the people. Today in the town of David a Savior has been born to you; he is Christ the Lord. This will be a sign to you: You will find a baby wrapped in cloths and lying in a manger." Suddenly a great company of the heavenly host appeared with the angel, praising God and saying, "Glory to God in the highest, and on earth peace to men on whom his favor rests" (Luke 2:8-14).

That is the reason why we celebrate the birth of Christ at Christmas. God had provided a way for humans to secure a place in Heaven other than being good enough. That way is someone. God's plan is a plan we would never think of and it is fair and just. To meet His standards of righteousness, which is necessary to go to Heaven, <u>He would replace our deeds of unrighteousness with the righteousness of Jesus Christ</u>. There is only one condition that we must meet. That is how simple it is. We must accept Jesus Christ to save us—to be our Savior—rather than our trying to save ourselves.

Since it is impossible for us to meet all of God's standards the Gospel of Jesus Christ is Good News because God can't pretend that sin doesn't exist. He didn't look at mankind and make an excuse for our sins. But in His great love for mankind He could do something about our sins and our sinful nature. He could pay the price for our sins Himself. That is a fair plan! And that is exactly what happened.

The blood of Jesus Christ has redeemed us. Jesus lived a perfect life then died as a sacrifice to pay the penalty for our sins. There is only one condition for His sacrifice to apply to my life! I must believe and accept God's offer.

If we will believe in His plan God does a wonderful thing: He credits our side of the ledger account with the righteousness of Jesus Christ. In the eyes of God the righteousness of Jesus Christ replaces our unrighteousness if we accept Him as our Savior. That is how God has taken care of our sins. That is how He has made us right and acceptable to be in His family. That is how we are included. He didn't change His standards in order to include us that we might go to Heaven. He made it possible for us to meet His standard by accepting Jesus Christ and His righteousness as our Savior.

> *But now a righteousness from God, apart from law* (our being able to keep all of God's commandments)*, has been made known, to which the Law and the Prophets testify. This righteousness from God comes through faith in Jesus Christ to all who believe* (accept Him as their Savior)*. There is no difference, for all have sinned and fall short of the glory of God, and are justified freely by his grace* (our salvation is a free gift from God) *through the redemption that came by Christ Jesus. God presented him as a sacrifice of atonement, through faith in his blood* (Romans 3:21-25a).

Did we deserve this free gift from God? No! His plan came into being because of His great love and mercy for His creation. We are special to Him, even though mankind rebelled against Him and His ways. His plan assures us of an eternity in Heaven rather than our being condemned to Hell, which is what we really deserve. How are you going to respond to such a gift from God? I hope you respond thankfully! Praise the Lord for His love and mercy!

A Point of Logic

My final word to you is simply a point of logic. Many people believe that most everyone goes to Heaven when they die. However, the Bible states that only those who accept Jesus Christ as their personal Savior go to Heaven. *Whoever believes in him* (Jesus Christ) *is not condemned, but whoever does not believe stands condemned already because he has not believed in the name of God's one and only Son* (John 3:18).

Only one of the above two ways to believe can be correct. If to believe that most everyone goes to Heaven turns out to be wrong, then to believe that way will cause us to miss Heaven. We will spend an eternity in Hell, a place far worse than anyone can imagine. However, to accept Jesus Christ as our personal Savior <u>will not</u> cause us to miss Heaven regardless of which way is correct—it <u>will not</u> do us any harm even if it is not correct.

One way of belief has the potential of terrible consequences, the other way, accepting the Gospel of Jesus Christ as presented in the Bible, has no gamble. One choice won't hurt me, regardless of what the truth is, the other choice could cost me my soul in Hell for an eternity if it is not the correct way to believe.

Since I don't have an option but to choose one or the other, logically, which is the wise choice for me to make? There is only one choice if we want to know for sure that we are going to Heaven when we die.

The Bible tells us a final Judgment Day is coming and that every person will be judged according to the way they lived this life of their own free will. God has given us a free will to make a choice between

Heaven and Hell. Our decision can be wonderful or it can be fearful and dreadful! You need to stop, listen, and consider your choice while the opportunity to do so is yours to make. Don't allow pro-crastination to delay your decision. More souls will go to Hell through procrastination than human arithmetic can calculate. Death has a way of striking unexpectedly. Then the last chance is gone. I am not playing on emotions, I am addressing intelligence, conscience, and free will. Soon we all pass over to that other side of the grave. To talk about death is not being morbid, it is just as rational as it is eventually inescapable. Ask the risen and living Savior Jesus Christ into your heart now. To possess Him is the only way to know for sure that you will be eternally saved and are going to Heaven.

A Critical Issue

The fact that there is even a possibility of a Heaven and Hell makes it far too critical of an issue for anyone to pass it off lightly by not thinking about it, ignoring it, or not trying to find out all that it involves. That is poor judgment. It is too costly a decision. I am talk-ing about something that will last for an eternity.

I do not want you to miss Heaven and you <u>do not</u> have to miss Heaven. However, the choice is yours. Like it or not you will make a choice. Repent (be sorry for and willing to turn from) the sinful nature that we all have and ask Jesus Christ into your heart as your personal Savior and Lord. If you are sincere and mean it from the heart you will experience a spiritual rebirth. It is not necessary to understand what all this means. You will know that it happened and you will be in the Kingdom of God and on your way to Heaven.

God knows your heart and is not as concerned with your words as He is with the attitude of your heart. The following is a suggested prayer for you: *Lord Jesus, I want to know You personally. Thank You for dying on the cross for my sins. I open the door of my life and receive You as my Savior and Lord. Thank You for forgiving me of my sins and giving me eternal life. Take control of the throne of my life. Make me the kind of person You want me to be.* If this prayer expresses the desire of your heart, pray this prayer right now, and Christ will come into your life as He promised.

If you pray this or a similar prayer I would suggest that you find others that you can tell of your decision to follow Jesus Christ. Ask the Lord to lead you to a church of Christians where you can study the Bible to learn His Word, worship, have fellowship and grow in your Christian life. To serve the One who made all creation and has all power over creation is the most wonderful life anyone can have while living this life on Earth. It is the enemy and the world that has duped us into thinking otherwise.

The Bible promises eternal life in Heaven to all who receive and remain faithful to Jesus Christ. *And this is the testimony: God has given us eternal life, and this life is in his Son. He who has the Son has life; he who does not have the Son of God does not have life. I write these things to you who believe in the name of the Son of God so that you may know that you have eternal life* (I John 5:11-13).

I am still serving the Lord on the mission field in Kenya, East Africa. I can be contacted through Christian Life Outreach, 6438 E. Jenan Dr., Scottsdale, AZ 85254.

One of the most successful programs we established in our ministry to help the poor and needy in Africa has been the school of nursing. Upon graduation from the intensive two and one half years of training, along with plenty of clinical work, the students would be considered as a registered nurse, specializing in general nursing, public and community health, and midwifery. Many of them must do the work of a general practitioner in the rural areas, being the only health provider for the poor and needy in the area.

As you can imagine, many students come from poor backgrounds, so it is necessary that we spend time to help raise financial funding for scholarships for needy nursing students. The nursing school serves three purposes: It educates Christian natives so they can be used to staff hospitals, clinics, and dispensaries; it helps move the native family of these trained nurses out of poverty and into a productive vocation; it establishes a good environment for Christian witness and needed health service to the respective tribes and communities.

If you might be interested in knowing more, or feel led to invest in the life of a young Kenyan Christian to be discipled for Christ and trained to serve Him through medicine and health care to the poor and needy people, please contact Christian Life Outreach at the above address. 100% of all contributions received for this project go directly to help the poor and needy. None of these funds are used for missionary support or administration expenses.

Additional copies of this book can be purchased at a Christian bookstore. The retail price is $14.95. Or you can order copies from:

Christian Life Outreach
6438 E. Jenan Drive
Scottsdale, AZ 85254
Phone: 1-480-998-4136
email: xnlifeout@aol.com

Please add $1.00 for postage and handling making a total of $15.95 for mail or email orders. All net prodeeds received from the sale of this book are used to help the poor and needy. My brother and I have chosen not to receive any financial compensation from the sale of this book.